Indians Along the Oregon Trail

Other Books from Webb Research Group
ISBN: 0-936738-

SILENT SIEGE-II: Japanese Attacks on North America in World War II (in 2 volumes) (-26-X) Bert Webber

Oregon's Great Train Holdup, Bandits Murder 4 — Didn't Get a Dime! (-31-6) Bert and Margie Webber

Who Were the People of Rajneeshpuram? (-30-8) Proceedings from Symposium. Edited by Bert Webber

The Rajneesh and the U.S. Postal Service; From Wasteland to an Oasis, the Buildings and Operation of a City (-29-4) Bert Webber

Ruch and Upper Applegate Valley, Oregon (-39-1) Marguerite Black

The Oregon & Overland Trail Diary of Mary Louisa Black in 1865 (-36-7) Introduction, Afterword and Genealogy by Marguerite Black

The Oregon Trail Dairy of Rev. Edward Evans Parrish in 1844 (-28-6) Parrish family genealogy appended. Edited by Bert Webber

The Oregon & California Trail Diary of Jane Gould in 1862 (-22-7) Edited by Bert Webber

The Oregon & Applegate Trail Diary of Welborn Beeson in 1853 (-21-9) Edited by Bert Webber

The Oregon Trail Emigrant Massacre of 1862 and Port-Neuf Muzzle-Loaders Rendezvous Massacre Rocks, Idaho (-23-5) Bert Webber

The Oregon Trail Memorial Half-Dollar (1926-1939) (-16-2) Bert Webber

Additional titles forthcoming.

INDIANS
ALONG THE
OREGON TRAIL

The Tribes of
Nebraska, Wyoming, Idaho, Oregon and Washington
Identified

BERT WEBBER, M.L.S.

WEBB RESEARCH GROUP

Published by: WEBB RESEARCH GROUP
Direct all inquiries to the distributor:

PACIFIC NORTHWEST BOOKS COMPANY
SAN 200-5263
P.O. Box 314   Medford, Oregon 97501

Postage stamps of Indian Head Penny, Crazy Horse, Conestoga Wagon,
Red Cloud courtesy U.S. Postal Service © U.S. Postal Service
1978, 1981, 1986, 1987

LIBRARY OF CONGRESS
Cataloging in Publications Data

Webber, Bert

Indians along the Oregon Trail : the tribes of Nebraska,
Wyoming, Idaho, Oregon, and Washington identified / Bert
Webber.

p. cm.
Bibliography: p.
Includes index.
ISBN 0-936738-38-3
1. Indians of North America—West (U.S.)—Social life
and customs. 2. Indians of North America—West (U.S.)—
Names. 3. Oregon Trail—History. 4. Frontier and pioneer
life—West (U.S.) I. Title.
E78.W5W39   89-5326
978—dc19   CIP

Table of Contents

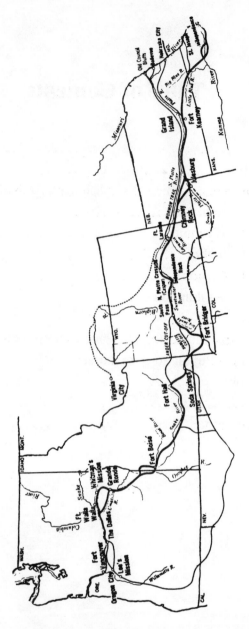

The Oregon Trail passed through Nebraska, Wyoming, Idaho, Oregon, with many pioneers visiting at Whitman Mission in Washington for a rest stop.

Preface

Although we have been aware for some years that available library reference books on Indians are somewhat obsolete, the fact really hit home in 1986. This was when Bill Yenne's excellent work *Encyclopedia of North American Indian Tribes* appeared. In doing a critical comparison for some librarians between the Yenne and the so-called "standard," John Reed Swanton's *Indian Tribes of North America*, especially the portions printed separately, *Indian Tribes of Washington, Oregon & Idaho* being Smithsonian Bureau of Ethnology Bulletin 145 (1952, now nearly forty years old), we found both authors listed many tribes in common though they did not necessarily have the same details. Further, each author had a few tribes the other did not. Nevertheless, each book served its purpose. Both are encyclopedic with usual short entries. Yenne offers maps and many full-page, full-color photographs in a large format page. He includes some historical essays. Bill Yenne's statistics, where he offers any, include 1985. Swanton included no art work, no maps and occasionally some very short historical notes.

Reaching back a tad further, we observe Frederick Webb Hodge's work of 1905, *Handbook of American Indians North of Mexico*, Smithsonian Bureau of Ethnology Bulletin 30. Hodge appears to have been the base from which Swanton started as data is substantially the same. Swanton however, does not appear to offer much after 1905 other than 1910 census, then in many entries gaps appear until 1937 populations. With this analysis we saw a need for a new reference work on Indians of the Pacific Northwest so we decided to launch a project that seeks to do these things:

7

Sacajewea, Teen-age mother and Guide

Young Shoshoni mother carrying her baby accompanied the Lewis and Clark expedition. Her interpretation skills provided safe passage through Shoshoni lands for the exploring party. Statue is in Washington Park, Portland, Oregon. It was unveiled at the Lewis and Clark Exposition, Portland in 1905.

—Photo courtesy Portland Archives & Records Center

Preface

1. Because of much new interest in the Oregon Trail, expand the book to include all four of the major Oregon Trail states by adding Nebraska and Wyoming
2. Update to most recent year the Bureau of Indian Affairs can supply data
3. Search for information to bridge gaps in earlier works
4. To brighten the book for general reading, instead of merely creating another short-entry encyclopedia, add feature-length historical essays
5. Eliminate obsolete usage such as designations of "creek" where the Geographic Names Board has decided the waterway was a "river." Update usage from calling a place a "post village" when we really mean the place had a post office
6. To make many place names "findable," we have inserted some references to locations on current highway maps
7. As we are aware of studies in progress and growing interest in postal history, we have tried to locate those early Indian villages that became permanent enough— even for a short period—to have a Post Office. We have provided the dates of operation for those offices when we could locate them. We have added ZIP Codes for those villages, now some of them are major cities, which are presently operational in the U.S. Postal Service.

While the editor has overcome a lot of hurdles with this project, there are some over which one does not seem able to jump. As historian Glen Cameron Adams wrote some years ago, Indians didn't come off too well when whites wrote the histories. Many of today's Indians seem to remember that for time has not changed Adams' observation because responses from tribal offices for this book did not come up to expectations. Nevertheless, there are many individuals who, realizing the scope of this project, dug in to assist in every way imaginable.

Anne Billeter, head of the Reference Department of Jackson County (Medford) Library, and her staff, seems to enjoy reference questions that tax the mind. We had a

9

number of these which they eagerly tackled, some requiring inter-library loans. Anne is assisted by Larry Calkins, Hardin Smith, Beverly Powell, Kate McGann, and Jan Gorden. I appreciate having this friendly and professional team available. Thank you all very much.

There is Richard Portal, my esteemed colleague and retired reference expert, who now lives in Salem, with whom I often burn midnight lamp with telephone to ear. Dick never tires of tough inquiry.

I was pleased to have the assistance of Steve Webber, a nephew, who is Archivist for the City of Portland.

Frank Swan, Director of Uinta County Library in Evanston, Wyoming, and his reference staff worked on a most intriguing question and helped identify a key item in the bibliography.

Then there is Glenn Barkhurst of Amanda Park, Washington. Glenn has been a willing and most able search-and-ye-shall-find associate for many years. Glenn was in the Coast Guard walking the beaches with a loaded rifle and a "war dog" on leash along the northwest coast in World War II. He, and others, were guarding against plausible Japanese landings. He retired to his favorite place, the rainy northwest coast, after years in Southern California. Barkhurst has a working knowledge of, and friends among the Indians especially on the Quinault Reservation. He witnessed the making of huge cedar sea-going canoes in 1988 and shared his information and his pictures with me.

There is a friendly, pioneering lady preacher who should be worth a TV special—Mrs. Paul D. (Deanna) Self-Price of the United Methodist Church at Beatty, Oregon. The Rev. Self-Price provided details of the land transfer back to the Klamath Tribe. Then she told how she, and for a while her single attending parishioner, would meet at the church on a Sunday morning, split the kindling and start the wood stove fire then together would hold a worship service, including singing, huddled around the stove.

Lynn Schonchin, a history teacher at Chiloquin High School, was kind enough to see me during a class break and to provide a copy of his manuscript about the Klamath

Indians. Much of what he presented is in no other source.

And there are many others whose few words here, a few there, when all put together have made this book. I humbly thank all of you for seeing me, for writing to me, for loaning your valued pictures to me, for making copies of newspaper clips for me, and for allowing me to talk to some of you, not previously met, on the telephone.

Additional thanks go to Leonard G. Lukens, an award-winning postal historian, for his work on this project and to Gene McCormick for providing examples of certain U.S. postage stamps on which the subjects are Indians.

To my wife, Margie, who handled many special parts of the book I offer my most sincere thanks. Margie selected the list of Chinook Jargon that is included then spent many hours with her very sharp blue pencil as copy editor.

A special thank you goes to Ken Asher and his staff at Maverick Publications, Bend, Oregon, who did the typesetting and manufacturing of this book.

Bert Webber
Central Point, Oregon
March 1, 1989

Introduction

There does not seem to be any way to fix an exact date when man first walked on the surface of North America, but Luther Cressman has found evidence of human life in the Pacific Northwest carbon-dated back some 9,000 years. Cressman also found evidence of human inhabitance along the coast to about AD 1000. He also stimulates the mind by advising that materials found at The Dalles, Oregon, and on Santa Rosa Island off the southwest California coast appear to be from 25,000 to 30,000 years old.

As to physical characteristic, the Indians of North America are Mongoloids who occupied the Asia mainland (an exception being the early occupants of Japan), which included Siberia and as far south as the Philippine Islands. These people's particular body shapes varied just as the shapes of bodies vary in the Negroid and Caucasian population. American Indians had great variations in their bodies also.

How did these "Native Americans" get here? Many papers have been presented on the theory of them having walked across a so-called land bridge between Siberia and Alaska. But the question is very easy to ask but thus far no one has been able to answer it. There is evidence that the human population of the Pacific Northwest came from the Northern Great Basin as much as 7,500 years ago. With water holes drying and vegetation dying, these people shifted south and westerly into the mountains. At least one researcher suspects the Pacific Northwest may have been peopled by those coming south along the coast but the greatest insurgence may have been westward over the Rocky Mountains and down the Snake River to the Columbia and continuing westward. How long did this migration require? Another excellent question but Cressman suggests we just

12

don't know. He did say that both sides of the Columbia River were occupied between 2,000 and 4,000 years ago. His evidence comes from the digs around The Dalles at the time the dam was being built and eventual carbon-dating of the findings.

The population was generally young of age. Cressman considers 1,000 children born in 1750 for a study. He suspects that half of them failed to live to age 21. Death was primarily due to childhood diseases and undoubtedly hypothermia in severe winters. Accordingly, if one reached age 30, he or she would be considered "old." Indians often had rotten teeth, as excavated skeletons reveal. They suffered from arthritis and rheumatism, broken bones and more than likely, many were malnourished.

While the editor makes no claims of being an anthropologist, we find the subject stimulating enough to encourage us to undertake this project.

As to "populations" shown in our tables, we note variance for given tribes among the researchers. For the serious reader, we cite many sources with support in the bibliography. Using the tribes along the Columbia River as an example, enumeration was very changeable because of intermingling of tribes going to the river to fish. Often so-called tribes, as reported, were merely seasonal fishing villages some very small, thus trappers, traders, explorers, even opportunists traveling through the area, recorded these Indians in different manners.

Various writers have used assorted phraseology in identifying the Federal government as source for population numbers. Commonly noted are "U.S. Office of Indian Affairs," and "U.S. Indian Office." Considering that the Bureau of Indian Affairs (B.I.A.) was created in 1824 long before any of these writers started their work, in an effort to avoid confusion in this book if the source was the Federal government, we merely show "B.I.A." in the tables.

Realizing that nearly all of the activity with Indians occurred between 1830 and 1880, we cross-checked our data with the 11th Edition of *Encyclopedia Britannica* (1910).

With respect to names of Indian Agencies and Indian

Reservations. Some writers refer to one when they meant the other but often both were on the same ground. The Agency was the location of the administrative offices for the reservation and was not necessarily the residence of others than the administrative staff—and some staff lived in nearby towns. The reservation was the residence grounds for the Indians. An example might be made of "Klamath." Here we find an Agency, a reservation as well as a military post (fort) but all were within the bounds of the reservation. (Buena Cobb Stone points out in her book *Fort Klamath, Frontier Post in Oregon 1863-1890* the fort never moved but changing county lines find it, historically, in Wasco County, was then part of Jackson County, then it was within Lake County and finally in Klamath County in 1882). In 1989, for "Klamath," the reservation is gone, the Agency buildings are primarily vacant many in tumbledown condition, and the fort is identified by a chain-link fence within which is a museum built like the original guard house, and graves for some hanged Modocs.

The Federal Government has a history of "hands-on" and "hands-off" matters dealing with Indians to the extent the editor expects to keep open files on this subject with the probability of an expanded edition at some future date. If readers find outstanding differences with what is contained here, please write to me about them for consideration in forthcoming works. As new information is sometimes limited to local media, if readers in particular areas care to send newspaper clippings—remember to insert name and date of the paper—we will welcome them. It is not possible to answer all personal letters but input is important and should be sent to the publisher.

Bureau of Indian Affairs
Establishment — Activities

Created as part of the War Department in 1824, the Bureau of Indian Affairs was eventually transferred to the Department of the Interior when Interior was established in 1849. The Snyder Act, 1921 (25 U.S.C. 13) provided substantive law for appropriations covering the conduct of activities by B.I.A. The scope and the character of the appropriations contained in Snyder were broadened by the Indian Reorganization Act of 1934 (25 U.S.C. 461 *et seq.*), the Indian Self-Determination and Education Assistance Act of 1975 (25 U.S.C. 450), and Title XI of the Education Amendments of 1978 (20 U.S.C. 2701 note).

The principal objectives of B.I.A. are to actively encourage and train Indian and Alaska Native peoples to manage their own affairs under the trust relationship to the Federal Government:

1. To facilitate with maximum involvement of Indian and Alaska Native people, full development of their human and natural resource potential
2. To mobilize all public and private aids to the advancement of Indian and Alaska Native people for use by them
3. To utilize the skill and capabilities of Indian and Alaska Native people in the direction and management of programs for their benefit.

In carrying out these objectives, B.I.A. works with Indian and Alaska Native people as well as with other Federal agencies and with State and local governments. The B.I.A. will also work with other interested groups in the development and implementation of effective programs for the advancement of Indians and Alaska Native peoples.

The B.I.A. seeks from all participating agencies adequate educational opportunities in public educational systems, and assists them in the creation and management of educational systems for their own benefit, or provides from Federal resources the educational systems needed. The B.I.A. actively promotes the improvement of the social welfare of Indians and Alaska Native peoples to obtain and provide needed social and community development programs and services. Further, work with them in the development and implementation of programs for their economic advancement and for full utilization of their natural resources consistent with the principles of resource conservation.

B.I.A. also acts as Trustee for their lands and moneys held in Trust by the United States, assisting them to realize maximum benefits from such resources.

CHAPTER 1

NEBRASKA

Arapaho

Important tribe of the Algonquin family associated with the Cheyenne since the 18th Century. They call themselves "Inuñaina" meaning "people-of-their-own-kind" or "our people." Known for friendliness probably due to their historical desire to trade. A religious people, did not like war. (See Wyoming)

Arikara

Apparently known in Nebraska during some prehistoric period, associated with the Skidi Pawnee. (See N. Dakota)

Cheyenne

"Sahaiyena" (French Canadian). Also from a Dakota term meaning "people of alien speech," or, "red talkers."
Also called:

> A-was-she-tan-qua, Hidatsa name (Long, 1791).
> Báhakosin, Caddo name, meaning "striped
> arrows."
> Dog Indians, so called sometimes owing to
> confusion of the name with the French word
> *chien.*
> Dzitsi'stäs, own name.
> Gatsalghi, Kiowa Apache name.
> Hitäsi'na or Itasi'na, Arapaho name,
> meaning "scarred people."
> I-sonsh'-pu-she, Crow name.
> Itah-Ischipahji, Hidatsa name (Maximilian, 1843).
> I-ta-su-pu-zi, Hidatsa name, meaning "spotted
> arrow quills."
> Ka'neaheawastsik, Cree name meaning "people
> with a language somewhat like Cree."
> Nanoniks-kare'niki, Kichai name.

Niere'rikwats-kûni'ki, Wichita name.
Päganävo, Shoshoni and Comanche name,
    meaning "striped arrows."
Säk'o'ta, Kiowa name.
Scarred Arms, from a misinterpretation of the
    tribal sign.
Sha-hö, Pawnee name.

Location: Earlier from Minnesota and Dakotas but forced to become nomadic by raiding Sioux. Found as far west as Rocky Mountains of eastern Wyoming.

History: Traditionally cooperated with the other plains tribes especially the Arapaho and were unfriendly with the Sioux. Encountered in 1680 by LaSalle in Minnesota, later migrated westward and settled in North Dakota. Apparently the Cheyennes were farm-oriented and raised corn. As the tribe moved it left agrarian pursuits and took up buffalo hunting, probably having been pushed out by the Sioux. They settled in South Dakota but about 1880 a contingent moved south to the Arkansas River. Later, under treaty arrangements, were moved to Indian Territory that became Oklahoma. In the meantime, the northern branch settled their differences with the Sioux then joined forces for attacks against white assumption.

A large group under Chief Crazy Horse attended the mass gathering of tribes in Montana, reportedly the largest Indian encampment in North American history. The Cheyenne were there as "guests" of the Sioux. On June 15, 1876, Colonel George A. Custer attacked the mass near the banks of the Little Big Horn River. Due to Custer's errors in judgment, the U.S. Army's 7th Cavalry met disaster and was killed to the last man by the Indians. Cheyennes harassed settlers until 1879. Major data on Cheyenne is in references to South Dakota.

Population: The Cheyennes were split on to several reservations.

1970   2,100 Northern Cheyenne Agency and Reservation in
            Montana
       6,674 Cheyenne-Arapaho Reservation, Oklahoma

1985 3,177 Northern Cheyenne Agency and Reservation in
        Montana
      5,220 Cheyenne-Arapaho Reservation, Oklahoma
1987 (See Appendix)

Names by which remembered: The name preserved by
the name of city that is State Capitol of Wyoming and by a
river in S. Dakota; counties in Colorado, Nebraska, Kansas.
The Cheyenne Mountains and canyons in Colorado and a
river in N. Dakota spelled "Sheyenne." There are other
remembrances of the name which include Cheyenne Wells,
Colorado and Sheyenne, a town in N. Dakota as well as
places in Oklahoma and in Texas.

Comanche
Believed to have lived in or near western Nebraska
before moving south. (See Texas)

Dakota
More commonly known as Sioux ("Nadouessioux").
The Dakotas are not known to have settled permanently in
Nebraska but raided constantly from the north. (See S.
Dakota)

Fox
Mesquaki, Muskwaki, "red earth people"; Utugamig,
"people of another shore." Of the Algonquin linguistic
group.
Locations and history: Originally Lake Winnebago,
Wisconsin, related to the Sauks, the Foxes driven from
homesteads on south shore Lake Superior by Chippewas.
Settled near Green Bay, Wisc., eventually migrating south-
westward into southeastern Nebraska. In 1842 moved to
Kansas later to Iowa where they purchased land on the Iowa
River in Tama County where they live today as farmers and
have assumed customs of whites, except they speak their
own language at home. Tribal Council of local government.
Known for tribal unity. There does not seem to be any
connections by which the name is remembered. There are

many towns, villages, creeks, post offices with this name, but these seem to have been named for the animal.

Population:

```
1985     56 Foxes and Sauks in Kansas
      1,041 Foxes and Sauks in Oklahoma
        745 Foxes and Sauks in Iowa
          0 Foxes and Sauks in Nebraska (Yenne)
1987  (See Appendix)
```

Iowa

From Minnesota, accompanied the Omahas who later went together into South Dakota and finally into Nebraska but later settled in State of Iowa.

Kansa

(Kaw) "south wind people." "Escanaques"

Linguistic group: Siouan-Dehegiha

Location: Eastern Nebraska and northeast Kansas, primarily Kansas. Ceded their tribal land in Nebraska to U.S. in Treaty of 1825 then moved primarily into Kansas.

Kiowa

Appear to have been located along the western border of Nebraska but later followed the Comanche to Oklahoma (which see).

Missouri

Linguistic group: Algonquin

Located mostly in Missouri but driven from their lands by the Sauk and Fox, remnants of the tribe settled to the south of the Platte River in villages. Closely associated with the Otos (which see). (See also Missouri)

Names by which remembered: Missouri River; State; City, Mo. Also Missouri City, Texas and Missouri Valley, Iowa.

Omaha

"Maha"—"Upstream people" or "those-who-go-against-the-wind." Also called:

20

Ho'-ma-ha, Winnebago name.
Hu-úmûi, Cheyenne name.
Oni'ha, Cheyenne name, meaning "drum beaters" (?).
Puk-tis, Pawnee name.
U'-aha, Pawnee name.

Linguistic group: Siouan

Location: In northeastern Nebraska in Elkhorn Valley after migrating from Missouri to Iowa, Minnesota, S. Dakota thence to Nebraska where they permanently settled for about 200 years until removed to reservation in Thurston County in 1856.

History: Noted for being probably the most friendly toward whites, but within the tribe there was strong, stern leadership. Blackbird, a tyrannical and powerful chief killed those whom he did not like, often with arsenic which he obtained and learned about from traders. Tribe decimated by smallpox about 1800. Other tribal leaders often sat with whites in conference and urged this tribe to accept the white man's form of government and manners of civilized life.

According to strong and circumstantial traditions, Omahas and others belonging to the same group formerly lived on the Ohio and Wabash Rivers. It is said that the Quapaw separated from the general body first, going down the Mississippi, but it is more likely that they were left behind by the others and later moved to the river. The Osage remained on Osage River, and the Kansa continued on up the Missouri, but the Omaha, still including the Ponca, passed north inland as far as the Pipestone Quarry in Minnesota, afterward forced west by the Dakota, into what is now South Dakota. There the Ponca separated from them and the Omaha settled on Bow Creek, in the present Nebraska. They continued from that time forward in the same general region, the west side of the Missouri River between the Platte and the Niobrara, but in 1855 moved to Dakota County, Nebraska. In 1854 they sold all of their lands except a portion kept for a reserve, and then sold a part for use by the Winnebagos (which see). In 1882, through the efforts of Miss Alice C. Fletcher, they were granted lands in severalty with prospects of citizenship, and

Miss Fletcher was given charge of the ensuing allotment.
Population:

1780	2,800 (Mooney, 1928)
1802	300 (reduced by smallpox)
1804	600 (estimate)
1829	1,900 (estimate)
1843	1,600 (estimate)
1851	1,349 (Schoolcraft)
1857	1,200 (Burrows)
1880	1,200 (U.S. Census)
1906	1,228 (B.I.A.)
1910	1,105 (U.S. Census)
1923	1,440 (B.I.A.)
1930	1,103 (U.S. Census)
1932	1,684 (B.I.A.)
1970	1,300 (Yenne)
1987	(See Appendix)

Names by which remembered: Omaha (city), Omaha
Beach (WW2 invasion beach in France). Omaha Indian
Reservation, many small places in Arkansas, Georgia,
Illinois, Texas, Kentucky and Virginia.

Oto

(Otoe) also: "Otto," "Otenta," "Otetoe," "Otheues,"
"Othoe," "Othonez," "Ottoes," "Otteaus"—the
"leachers." Also called:

Che-wae-rae, own name.
Matokatági, Shawnee name.
Motútatak, Fox name.
Wacútada, Omaha and Ponca name.
Wadótata, Kansa name.
Watohtata, Dakota name.
Watútata, Osage name.

Linguistic group: Siouan
Location: In eastern Nebraska along or close to the
Platte River near confluence with Missouri River—four
villages—probably between 1841-1880.
Tribal history: From maps of the Marquette expedi-

tion, it would seem at the time the maps were drawn in 1673, the Oto were some distance up the Des Moines River. Their name was often coupled with that of related Iowa who lived north of them, but they always seem to have occupied a distinct area. Shortly after this time they moved to the Missouri and by 1804 had established their towns on the south side of the Platte River not far from its mouth. According to native traditions, this tribe, and the Missouri were anciently one people with the Winnebago, but moved southwest from them, and then separated from the Iowa at the mouth of the Iowa River and from the Missouri at the mouth of the Grand River. Their language proves that they were closely related to these tribes whether or not the separations occurred in the manner and at the places indicated. Their split with the Missouri is said to have been brought about by a quarrel between two chiefs over the seduction of the daughter of one by the son of the other. From this circumstance the Oto are supposed to have derived their name. In 1700 they were, according to Le Sueur, on Blue Earth River near the Iowa. It is probable they moved into the neighborhood of the Iowa or Missouri at several different times, but their usual position was clearly intermediate along a north-south line. In 1680 two Oto chiefs came to visit La Salle in Illinois and reported that they had traveled far enough west to fight with people using horses, evidently Spaniards, a report that tends to validate their early westward ventures.

By treaties signed July 15, 1830, and October 15, 1836, they and the Missouri ceded all claims to land in Missouri and Iowa, and by another signed September 21, 1833, the two ceded all claims to land south of the Little Nemaha River. By a treaty signed March 15, 1854, they gave up all their lands except a strip 10 miles wide and 25 miles long on the waters of Big Blue River, but when it was found that there was no timber on this tract it was exchanged on December 9 for another tract taken from the Kansas Indians. In a treaty signed August 15, 1876, and amended March 3, 1879, they agreed to sell 120,000 acres off the western end of their reserve. Finally, a treaty signed March

3, 1881, provided the consent of the tribe being obtained, for the sale of all of the remainder of their land in Kansas and Nebraska, and the selection of a new reservation. Consent to the treaty was recorded May 4 and the tribe moved the following year to a new reservation which was in Oklahoma southwest of Arkansas River on Red Rock and Black Bear Creeks, west of the Pawnee area. This move to Oklahoma is said to have been due to a spontaneous division of the tribe which resulted in two bands: The Coyotes, who were conservative and moved in 1880. The Quakers, progressives, moved in 1882.

The Oto was a lesser tribe with a demonstrated history of many moves and a continuing struggle against stronger neighbors. Finally, it would appear the tribe just gave up, sold out and took to reservation life in Oklahoma. Whether the tribe's population was mostly cut back by the wars or smallpox is debatable.

Population:

1780	900 (Mooney, 1928)
1805	500 (Lewis and Clark)
1833	1,300 (Catlin)
1849	900 (Burrows, includes Missouri)
1862	708
1867	511
1886	344
1906	390
1910	332 (U.S. Census)
1930	627 (1 in Nebraska)
1937	756 (in Oklahoma)
1950	930 (Yenne)
1985	1,231 (Yenne)
1987	(See Appendix)

Names by which remembered: Otoe County, Otoe (village), Nebraska. Also towns in Iowa and Missouri.

Pawnee

"Chahiksichiks" ("men of men" or "last of men"), 'Pani," "Pana," "Panama," "Paneas," "Panzas," "Pariki" ("horn" of hair—a dressing of fat and paint to stiffen

the hair, thus hair stood on end in horn-shape).
Also known as:

> Ahihinin, Arapaho name, meaning "wolf people."
> Awahi, Caddo and Wichita name.
> Awahu, Arikara name.
> Awó, Tonkawa name, originally used by the Wichita.
> Chahiksichahiks, meaning "men of men," applied to
> themselves but also to all other tribes whom they
> considered civilized.
> Dárazhazh, Kiowa Apache name.
> Harahey, Coronado documents (somewhat uncertain).
> Ho-ni'-i-tani-o, Cheyenne name, meaning "little wolf people."
> Kuitare-i, Comanche name, meaning "wolf people."
> Paoneneheo, early Cheyenne name, meaning "the ones with
> projecting front teeth."
> Páyi, Kansa form of the name.
> Pi-ta'-da, name given to southern tribes (Grinnell, 1923).
> Tse-sa do hpa ka, Hidatsa name meaning "wolf people."
> Wóhesh, Wichita name.
> Xaratenumanke, Mandan name.

Pawnee were one of the principal tribes of Caddoan linguistic group. The Arikara tribe was an offshoot.

Subdivisions: The Pawnees consisted in reality of four tribes, or four known in historic times, viz: The Chaui or Grand Pawnee, the Kitkehahki or Republican Pawnee, the Pitahauerat or Tapage Pawnee, and the Skidi or Skiri Pawnee. The first three speaking the same dialect and being otherwise more closely connected with one another than the last. The Kitkehahki embraced two divisions, the Kitkehahki proper and the Little Kitkehahki. Murie gives two others, the Black Heads and Karikisu, but Lesser and Weltfish (1932) state the first was a society and the second the name of the women's dance or ceremony before corn planting. The Pitahauerat consisted of the Pitahauerat proper and the Kawarakis, sometimes said to be villages.

These subdivisions were in these locations: Throughout Nebraska in four principal locations:

> 1) Chaui (Grand Pawnee), south bank of Platte River new
> Schuyler.

2) Kitkehaki (Republican Pawnee), south side Republican River near Red Cloud.
3) Skidi (Loup/Wolf Pawnee), Loup Fork of Platte River.
4) Pitahauerat (Noisy Pawnee), on Platte River near Grand Pawnee.

History: Some Pawnee trace their origin to the southwest, some to the east, and some claim always to have lived in the country with which later history associates them. The first white men to meet any members of these tribes were the Spaniards under Coronado in 1541. French explorers heard of them early in the eighteenth century and French traders were established among them before the middle of it. The Spaniards of New Mexico became acquainted with them at about this time on account of raids which the Pawnee conducted in search of horses. They lay somewhat out of the track of the first explorers from the east, and in consequence suffered less decline in numbers through white influences than did many of their neighbors. They were considerably reduced however, because of wars with surrounding tribes particularly the Dakota. Although some early traders and trappers were treated harshly, their relations with the United States Government were friendly from the first. They regularly furnished scouts for the frontier armies.

Of interest is the Canadian Ordinance of April 13, 1709, in which enslavement of Negroes and Pawnee was recognized (Charleviox, v.224, 1871). The Pawnee does not seem to have suffered much from this traffic, which was lucrative for the sellers, but had to be discontinued due to animosities it generated.

Lewis & Clark estimated there were 10,000 Pawnee when the tribes united near Fullerton to become the Great Pawnee Nation. Their population decreased alarmingly due to white influence. This included measles, venereal diseases, liquor, then the cholera epidemic of 1849, a by-product from the overland migration along the Oregon Trail. Over the years the tribes ceded their land to the federal government and in 1848 sold an 80-mile strip including Grand Island. By 1875 all their land was gone and the tribe moved to the Indian Territory in Oklahoma.

It was rare when the Pawnee and whites fought against each other. When the Union Pacific was constructing its rail line westward, Pawnee guards ("The Pawnee Battalion") were hired by the railroad as protection from raids by hostile tribes. Mainly farmers, the Pawnee were experienced in growing beans, corn, melons of several varieties, as well as tobacco. The women did most of the work. For variety in diet, this tribe looked for wild fruit and edible greens as well as hunted local small game. In summer months the villages were mostly inhabited by the women as the men were away for annual buffalo hunting.

Many of the resident tribes of the plains lived in earthen houses (lodges). These were circular from about 20 to more than 60 feet in diameter and accommodated several families. These buildings were constructed with poles as upright members then braced with limbs of trees, smaller branchs, then plastered with mud in which grass was mixed for strength. When dry, the "house" was able to withstand fierce winds and thunderstorms. These lodges were not very high off the ground and had floors about three feet below the outside ground level. The ceiling (roof) had a center hole for a vent through which smoke from the fire that was directly beneath passed. A good fire was guaranteed as the building had no windows but the "door" was facing east and was from ten to 30 feet in length, an entrance "tunnel," at ground level. This tunnel was "engineered" to be about one third the length of the diameter of the lodge.

Population:

1702	2,000 families (Iberville)
1780	10,000 (Mooney, 1928)
1838	10,000 (Dunbar)
1849	4,500 (following cholera epidemic)
1856	4,686
1879	1,440 (after removal to Oklahoma)
1910	633 (U.S. Census)
1923	773 (B.I.A.)
1930	730 (U.S. Census)
1970	1,149 (Yenne)

1985   1,997 (Yenne)
1987   (See Appendix)

Names by which remembered: Pawnee county and a
city in Nebraska. Pawnee Road, a major thoroughfare in
City of Omaha. Pawnee, Oklahoma.

Ponca

"Panka," "Punka," ("sacred head"). Also called:

Dihit, Li-hit' or Rihit, Pawnee name.
Kan'ka, Winnebago name.
Tchiaxsokush, Caddo name.

Linguistic group: Siouan, Dhegiha sub-group
Location and history: The early life of the Ponca seems
to have run parallel with the Omaha. They are said to have
separated from the latter at the mouth of White River, S.
Dak., and to have moved west into the Black Hills but to
have rejoined the Omaha later. These two tribes and the
Iowa then descended the Missouri together as far as the
mouth of the Niobrara, where the Ponca remained while the
Omaha established themselves below on Bow Creek. They
were moved west by the federal government in 1858, but
returned in 1865 by the government to traditional grounds;
but in 1858 treaty at Fort Laramie, Poncas lost their lands
to the Sioux, who quickly decimated them. In 1877 moved
to Oklahoma Indian Territory. When Oklahoma became a
state (1906) the Ponca lands were divided among those in
Oklahoma.
Population:

1780   800 (Mooney, 1928)
1804   200 (Lewis and Clark mention smallpox epidemic)
1829   600
1842   800
1871   747
1877   700 (Hodge)
          19 (in Nebraska—Hodge)
         681 (in Oklahoma—Hodge)
1903   236 (in Nebraska—Hodge)

```
1906    263 (in Nebraska—Swanton)
        570 (in Oklahoma—Swanton)
1910    875 (total—U.S. Census)
1923  1,381 (B.I.A.)
1930    939 (U.S. Census)
1937    397 (Nebraska—U.S. Census)
        825 (Oklahoma—U.S. Census)
1985  2,272 (Yenne)
1987  (See Appendix)
```

Names by which remembered: Ponca City, Oklahoma; Ponca, Nebraska.

Santee Sioux (See Sioux)

Sauk (See Fox)

Sioux
Dakota, Lakota, Nakota, Otchente Chakowie, Nadowessisoix, Nadoweisiw (meaning, "enemy" or "snake").

Sub-groups: Santee (eastern): M'dewakanton, Santee, Sisseton, Wahpekute, Wahpeton Teton (western): Blackfoot Sioux (not to be confused with Blackfeet); Brule, Hunkpapa, Miuneconjou, Oglala, Sans Arc, Teton, Two Kettle.

Location: Mid-western plains especially Nebraska, Wyoming to Rocky Mountains and into Canada in direction of Lake Winnipeg.

Linguistic group: Siouan

History: Early agrarian tribe; pottery makers. Later, these Indians roamed for many years, but on being pushed by settlers proved to be quite hostile and fought the intruders. Life was a great struggle against the encroachment of whites. Culminating scraps were against Colonel George A. Custer in 1876 at Battle of the Little Big Horn River in Montana, the incident at Wounded Knee, South Dakota, in 1890 when U.S. troops massacred about 200 Indians, then in 1973. In this late year, about 200 members of what was called The American Indian Movement lead by Dennis Brooks and Russell Means, stormed and took over the reservation village of Wounded Knee and set up the

Independent Ogala Sioux Nation as a means to bring the plight of Indians to the attention of the federal government. The Indians sought Congressional investigation of Indian treatment in general. Federal Marshals surrounded the village, starting a 69-day siege on February 27, 1973. Finally, on May 8, the Indians surrendered after two of their number were killed and one of the federal marshals was wounded, on promises of negotiations of grievances. Due to the period in history when this occurred, it is the only Indian "battle" to be covered by live television—so far!

The overall tribe, with its many sub-divisions and covering such a huge area, had varied customs. No single statement will fit all. Some settled in villages and farmed corn as their main crop. Their diet was augmented by buffalo, other game animals and fish. Others were nomadic and moved entire villages as necessary in pursuit of food. (Another group of Sioux were in North and South Carolina as well as parts of Virginia; along the gulf coast in Mississipi.)

Lewis and Clark reported meeting most of the Sioux tribes. With the pressure for removal of the Indians from the path of westward-bound pioneers and 'way settlers, the federal government moved the Sioux to reservations in the Dakotas, Nebraska and Montana.

Chief Crazy Horse of the Sioux

Determined to thwart encroachment of the whites, Crazy Horse proved a worthy tactition and determined fighter participating in the Fetterman Massacre and the Wagon Box Fight as well as Custer's defeat at the Little Big Horn River. He surrendered only when his tribe was without food and weak from the cold winter. He was killed while confined at Fort Robinson some writers claiming he was trying to escape while others contend he was murdered.

—Courtesy U.S. Postal Service
© U.S. Postal Service 1981

Population:

    1950   51,645 throughout the United States
            2,503 in Canada

1985   18,754 Oglala Sioux (Pine Ridge Reservation)
       11,685 Teton Sioux (Rosebud Reservation)
        8,443 Teton Sioux (Standing Rock Reservation)
        5,150 Teton Sioux (Cheyenne River Agency)
        1,082 Teton Sioux (Lower Brule Reservation)
        4,043 Sisseton Sioux (Sisseton Reservation)
        2,355 Yankton Sioux (Crow Creek Reservation)
        2,929 Yankton Sioux (Yankton Reservation)
        3,162 Sioux in North Dakota
          422 Sioux in Nebraska
        5,073 Sioux in Montana
          639 Sioux in Minnesota
1987   (See Appendix)

Names by which remembered: Sioux Center, Sioux City, Sioux Rapids, Iowa; Sioux Falls, S. Dakota.

Chief Red Cloud of the Sioux

Red Cloud demanded the abandonment of two army forts along the Bozeman Trail and fought to protect his territory in what is called "Red Cloud's War" in 1866. This included an attack on Fort Laramie but he was finally beaten and signed a treaty (1868) which guaranteed the abandonment of the Bozeman Trail forts and provided a huge reservation. Red Cloud was highly respected, led delegations to Washington, D.C. on behalf of his people.

—Photo from Bert Webber collection

Winnebago

"Puabs" ("fetid") "dis-favored ones"

Linguistic group: Siouan

Location: Migrated to Nebraska from Wisconsin to Minnesota then to Nebraska in 1865 to the Winnebago Indian Reservation in Thurston County. A sub-group remained in Wisconsin.

History: The Winnebagos were native to the area of Green Bay, Wisconsin, and got along well with the French, then the British, but the encroachment of American settlers disturbed them. They lost the Winnebago War of 1827 then gave all their lands to the government—migrated into Minnesota. Their losses in the war were great, followed by smallpox epidemic of 1832 which further reduced their numbers. They were nearly destitute after the Sioux battle at their reservation near Crow Creek, South Dakota, and in 1863-64 vacated the reservation and joined their blood-brothers, the Omahas, on their reservation in Thurston County, Nebraska.

In 1865 the Omahas negotiated with the federal government whereby the government would buy about 97,000 acres from the Omahas then return the land to the Winnebagos as their permanent reservation. This was finalized in 1865. In 1887 the land was alloted 160 acres to the head of each family as many were farmers. By 1939 much of the land was rented to white farmers and some had been sold. These deals were supervised by the superintendent of the reservation. Winnebagos have always been artistic, especially with designs in weaving as well as beadwork. They also make bracelets, rings, rugs and moccasins.

Population:

1822	5,800
1833	4,350
1970	1,813
1985	1,183 (Yenne)
1987	(See Appendix)

Names by which remembered: Winnebago (town); reservation; popular brand of recreational vehicle.

CHAPTER 2

WYOMING

Arapaho

Tiraphiu, larapihu ("buyer"/"trader"). The most versatile traders of the plains region.

Linguistic group: Algonquin

Also known as:

Ahya'to, Kiowa name.

Ano's-anyotskano, Kichai name.

Betidee, Kiowa Apache name.

Detseka'yaa, Caddo name, signifying "dog eaters."

Dog Eaters.

E-tah-leh, Hidatsa name, signifying "bison path Indians."

Hitanwo'iv, Cheyenne name, signifying "cloud men" or "sky men."

Inûna-ina, own name, signifying "our people" or, "people of their own kind."

Ita-Iddi, Hidatsa name (Maximilian).

Kaninahoish, Chippewa name.

Komséka-Ki'ñahyup, former Kiowa name, signifying "men of the worn-out leggings."

Kun na-nar-wesh or Gens des Vach[es], by Lewis and Clark (1804)

Mahpíyato, Dakota name, signifying "blue cloud."

Nia'rhari's-kûrikiwa'ahûski, Wichita name.

Säretika, Comanche and Shonshoni name, signifying "dog eaters"; the Pawnee, Wichita, and Ute names were forms of this.

Location: The Arapaho occupied a number of different regions in history, but after they crossed the Missouri River they became closely identified with northeastern Wyoming. The main (northern) part of the tribe lived many years in Wyoming and were finally given a reservation. In 1804, the tribe seems to have maintained their home between the forks of the Platte River in alliance with the Cheyenne and Oglala Sioux, later as far east as Grand Island.

Subdivisions: The Arapaho recognized five main divisions, which were evidently originally distinct tribes. (1)

Nákasine'na, Báachinena, or Northern Arapaho; (2) Náwunena, or Southern Arapaho; (3) Aä'ninena, Hitúnena, Atsina, or Gros Ventres of the Prairie, today usually reckoned as a distinct tribe (see Montana); (4) Bäsawunena, principally with the Northern Arapaho; and (5) Hánahawunena, or Aanû'nhawa, later incorporated with the Northern Arapaho. The corresponding names given by Kroeber (1902) are: Hinanae'ina^n (Arapaho proper), Nä^n-waҫcinä'äna^n (evidently Southern Arapaho), Hitoune'na^n (Gros Ventres), Bääsa^{n}wuune'na^n, and Ha^{n}anaxawuune'a^n. Kroeber also states that four more divisions recognized in the tribe were evidently in reality divisions of the Hinanae'ina. These are: Wa^{n}xue'iҫci ("ugly people"), about Cantonment, Okla.; Haxaa^{n}ҫcine'na^n ("ridiculous men"), on the South Canadian, Okla.; Baa^{n}tciine'na^n ("red willow men"), in Wyoming; and a fourth whose name has been forgotten. The following are relatively modern local bands of the Arapaho: Forks-of-the-River Men, Bad Pipes, Greasy Faces, Wáquithi, Aqáthine'na, Gawunena, Háqihana, Säsábäithi, of which the first three were among the Northern Arapaho.

History: According to tradition, the Arapaho were once sedentary and seem to have lived in the Red River Valley, but migrated southwest across the Missouri at some time prior to the passage of that stream by the Cheyenne. Sometime afterward the Atsina separated from the rest, possibly cut off from the main body by the Crow, and moved off to the north. Within the last century the rest of the tribe slowly divided into a northern and a southern branch, the Northern Arapaho living along the edges of the mountains at the headwaters of the Platte, while the Southern Arapaho continued on toward the Arkansas. About 1840 they made peace with the Dakota, Kiowa, and Comanche, but were at war with the Shoshoni, Ute, and Pawnee until they were confined to reservations. By the treaty of Medicine Lodge in 1867, the Southern Arapaho were moved to a reservation in Oklahoma along with the Southern Cheyenne. The Northern Arapaho were moved to a reservation on Wind River, Wyo., after making peace with the Shoshoni who occupied the same reserve. The Atsina were associated with the Assiniboin on Fort Belknap Reservation, Montana.

Population:

1780	3,000 (Mooney, 1928)
1894	2,638 (combined with Atsina)
1902	905
1904	899 (Northern Arapaho)
	859 (Southern Arapaho)*
1910	1,419 (combined—U.S. Census)
1923	921 (Northern Arapaho)
	833 (Southern Arapaho)*
1924	692 (Northern Arapaho—all time low)
1930	1,241 (combined—U.S. Census)
1937	1,164 (Northern Arapaho)
	2,836 (Southern Arapaho and Cheyenne)*
1950	1,189 (Southern Arapaho)*
1985	5,220 (combined)
1987	(See Appendix)

*In Oklahoma

Names by which remembered: A county and a mountain in Colorado. Towns in Nebraska, N. Carolina, Colorado, Wyoming, Oklahoma.

Bannock

Members of Bannock hunted in western Wyoming. (See Idaho)

Cheyenne

Along with the Arapaho, the Cheyenne ranged into eastern Wyoming from Nebraska and from S. Dakota. (See Nebraska)

Comanche

This tribe plausibly roamed in eastern Wyoming before their separation from the Shoshoni, but the Comanche eventually went south into Texas.

Crow

Crow occupied the area of the Yellowstone River and extended as far south as region of the Laramie and N. Platte Rivers of Wyoming. One authority (Swanton) suggests the Crow ranged as far south as Laramie—the present city. This seems doubtful due to extreme differences in terrain to which the Crow were accustomed. (See Montana)

Dakota
Hunting as well as war parties ranged into Wyoming but there have been no permanent settlements discovered. (See S. Dakota)

Kiowa
Appear to have been at the eastern edge of Wyoming, and in western Nebraska, before moving to Oklahoma.

Kiowa Apache
Associated with the Kiowa.

Pawnee
Primarily from Nebraska, the Pawnee sent hunting parties into eastern Wyoming. (See Nebraska)

Shoshoni
Western Wyoming was at one time the home of the Northern Shoshoni. (See Idaho)

Ute
Although Ute were primarily from Utah, bands of Ute entered Wyoming over the mountains on the south for hunting expeditions.

Chief Washakie of the Shoshoni

Chief Washakie was a friend of Jim Bridger and recognized that it was necessary to blend Indian philosophy and ways of doing things with the whites who were arriving in increasing numbers. Washakie was a fearless man to the point where hostile Indians kept their distance believing him invincible. He was proud that he never killed a white person and often helped whites with safe passage. He fully recognized that Indians could not stop advancing civilization and helped with obtaining land for the Wind River Reservation. In recognition, President Ulysses Grant sent a prize horse and saddle to the Chief. At age 96, he died on the reservation where there is a marker off Highway 287 near Fort Washakie, Wyoming. Having been made an Honorary Captain in the Army, on his death he was accorded a full military funeral.

—Photo from Bert Webber Collection

CHAPTER 3

IDAHO

Bannock
"Panaítu," "Bana'kwut" ("their own name")
Also called:

Diggers
Kutshundika (Buffalo eaters)
Penointikara (Honey eaters)
Shihopanaiti (Cottonwood Bannock)
Yambadika (Root eaters)
Waradika (Rye-grass seed eaters)
Ogoize, by the Kalispel
Panaiti
Pun-nush, by the Shoshoni
Robber Indians
Ush-ke-we-ah, by the Crow

Linguistic group: Uto-Aztecan, Shoshonean division (Northern Paiute sub-group)

Location and history: There were two geographic divisions, but references to the Bannock do not always note this distinction. The home of the chief division appears to have been southeast Idaho, from where they ranged into western Wyoming. The country actually claimed by the chief of this souther division, which seems to have been recognized by the treaty of Ft. Bridger, July 3, 1868, lay between lat. 42° and 45°, and between long. 113° and the main chain of the Rocky Mountains. It separated the Wihinasht Shoshoni of western Idaho from the Washaki band of Shoshoni of western Wyoming. They were found in this region in 1859, and they asserted that this had been their home in the past. Bridger (Ind. Aff. Rep., 363, 1859) had known them in this region as early as 1829. Bonneville found them in 1833 on Portneuf River near the present Fort Hall reservation. Many of this division affiliated with the

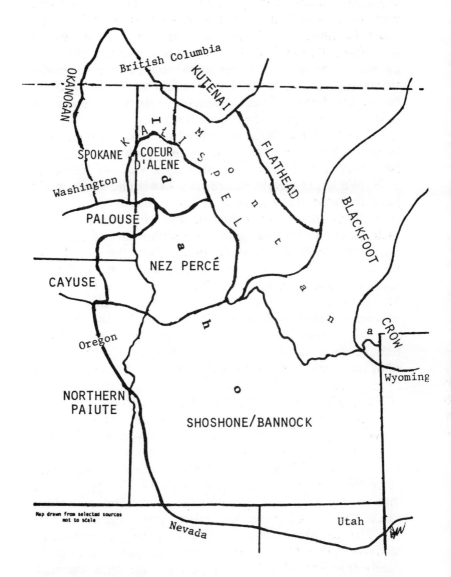

Traditional tribal territories of Eastern Washington, Eastern Oregon, Idaho, Western Montana, Northwest Wyoming.

Washaki Shoshoni, and by 1859 had extensively intermarried with them. Fort Hall reservation was set apart by Executive order in 1869. This is just west of the present city of Blackfoot. Six hundred Bannock as well as many Shoshoni agreed to stay there, however many decided to leave shortly thereafter. As late as 1874 an appropriation was made to enable the Bannock and Shoshoni, scattered to southeast Idaho, to be moved to the reservation.

The Northern Division of the Bannock was discovered living on the Salmon River in eastern Idaho by Governor Isaac Stevens and recorded in his Pacific Railroad Report of 1855. While not clearly established, Lewis and Clark might have included the Bannock with the Shoshoni unless, as more likely, these were called Broken Moccasin Indians in their mention. It's plausible the Salmon River (Northern) Bannock had crossed the mountains from the east due to pressures on them by the Siksika, which tribe claimed southwest Montana as theirs. On today's maps, the area in Montana would include Bozeman and nearby towns. Stevens reported the Northern Bannock had been hurt more by smallpox than by trouble with Siksikas. Hodge, writing in 1905, suggests that at one time, before these Indians got horses, all of the people of the tribe were combined in a central locality in southeastern Idaho. Although they had been neighbors of the Shoshoni, the Bannock's language differed.

The Bannock roved the countryside and tended to break up into groups. Both the men and women had strong physical stamina and thus there was no need for them to stay at home. They resembled the Shahaptian Nez Perce more than other Shoshonies. A study by Kroeber is clear that the language of the Bannocks at Fort Hall resembled that of the Ute rather than with other Shoshoneans.

The decrease in buffalo herds and the loss of hunting lands as well as the failure of the federal government to be timely in relief, accounted in part for the 1878 Bannock War. While the Nez Perce fought a running battle in 1877 with the whites, Bannocks were forced to sit out on the reservation on a congressional handout of only 2½ cents per person per day. The Bannocks were getting edgy.

During the summer, a liquored-up Bannock got into some difficulties with some teamsters. The Bannock got his gun then shot and wounded two of the whites. The Indian was arrested Nov. 23, 1877, but this stirred up the Indians to a point where an agency employee was killed. Troops were called. The murderer was pursued and captured. He was tried, then promptly hung. This episode so incensed the Indians that the commander of the troops determined the Indians had become a threat so he surrounded two Bannock camps in the bitter cold of January 1878. But the army had no way to house and feed its prisoners, thus the Indians were released.

Regrettably, the government, be it the army or the agency staff, could not feed the Indians. As the Bannocks had never really settled themselves on the reservation, they wandered off in the spring to their traditional "garden." This growing area was Camas Prairie, so named because wild camas root (a lily) grew there and was much prized as food. The Bannock Indian War of 1878 came about due to errors and misunderstanding about the prairie. Whites had moved in. Their cattle trampled the prairie and destroyed the crop. The Indians never intended to give up these lands or the privilege of gathering camas to the whites. In McConnel's *History of Idaho*, as well as in Rees' *Idaho, Chronology, Nomenclature, Bibliography*, is found the report that this war was precipitated by the ignorance of some government clerk who in transcribing the treaty replaced the unfamiliar name, "Camas Prairie," with "Kansas Prairie." Although because of this error there was no mention of the Camas Prairie in the treaty, it was understood that the makers of the treaty intended the Bannocks should be allowed to harvest their annual crop of camas. That was the Indians' understanding. No wonder they were angry when they found the cattle of the white men uprooting the food they prized so highly.

The Bannock chief, Buffalo Horn, was chiefly responsible for their going on the warpath. Since he had served under General Howard in the Nez Perce War and was

(Note: *Quamasia quamash*, the edible camas (bulbs) identified by bluish to white flowers. *Zygadenus veneosus*, "Death Camas" with cream-colored, green-striped flowers has deadly poisonous bulbs. —Ed.)

familiar with military tactics, he was a dangerous enemy to the whites. The band first attacked settlers on Camas Prairie, and then began a series of murders and raids on white persons living in southwestern Idaho. They successfully avoided a general engagement with the troops following them, although they were forced into a few brief and bloody battles, in one of which their leader, Buffalo Horn, was killed. The loss of their chief did more than anything else to break up the war, although some of the Indians, hoping to make an alliance with powerful Oregon tribes, refused to surrender even though General Howard was following closely. Finally, however, the troops succeeded in disorganizing the Indians, separating them into small bands for protection, thus the Indians made their way back to the "protection" of Fort Hall reservation.

For the sake of completeness, regarding the end of the Bannock Indian War, it should be acknowledged that General Howard's pursuit was relentless. The army captured about 1,000 Indians during the unmercifully sweltering days of August. The fight came to a quick end on September 5th where twenty Bannock lodges had been surrounded and suddenly attacked, killing all the women and children. Some sources suggest that Chief Buffalo Horn was killed by the army, however Rees wrote differently. Rees states all was not well within the leadership of the Indians, the Bannocks having been joined in the war by a confederacy of red men from most of the tribes of Idaho, eastern Oregon and Washington, even including old Chief Winnemucca of Nevada for a time. One Pahute Joe, who held a grudge against Buffalo Horn, tricked the chief into coming away from the group at the Battle of South Mountain (Owyhee County) where the chief was shot and killed. It is probably true that the outcome of the Bannock Indian War would have been quite different had not its chief been killed so near the onset.

Population:

    1829   8,000 (probably included Shoshoni—Bridger)
    1845   1,000 (Mooney, 1928)

1858	400+ (Forney)
1870	600 (Jones)
1885	425
1910	413 (U.S. Census)
1930	415 (U.S. Census)
1937	342 (Swanton)
1985	2,250 (Wind River Reservation, Wyoming)
1987	(See Appendix)

Names by which remembered: The Bannock Indian War; river; range of mountains; a county. Towns of Bannock in Kentucky and in Ohio do not appear to have been named for the tribe.

Coeur d'Alene (See Skitswish)

Kalispel (Calispel)
Camas, ("wearers of shell earrings")
Also called:

> Ak-min'-e-shu'-me, by the Crow ("the tribe that uses canoes")
> Camas People, a translation of Kalispel.
> Earring People, an English translation of Pend d'Oreilles
> Hanging Ears, English translation of Pend d'Oreilles
> Ni-he-ta-te-tup'i-o, Siksika name
> Papshpûn'lema, Yakima name ("people of the great fir trees")

Linguistic group: Salishan, interior division
Location: Along the Pend Oreille River and lake, Priest Lake and the lower end of Clark Fork River. Historians claim the Kalispel extended east to Thompson Lake and Horse Plains as well as to the Salmon River area of Canada. The Kalispel was also reported in the Flathead Lake and Missoula areas of Montana as well as in Washington in the Cusick area.
Subdivisions: (1) Upper Kalispel or Upper Pend Oreilles (in Montana from Flathead Lake and Flathead River to about Thompson Falls on Clark Fork River, including the Little Bitterroot, southward about to Missoula and northward to the International Boundary), with bands at Flathead Lake, near Kalispel, at or near Dayton, near Polson at the foot of the lake, and possibly one at Columbia

Falls. Some wintered along the Bitterroot River as well as at St. Ignatius in Montana.

(2) Lower Kalispel or Lower Pend Oreilles or Kalispel proper (from Thompson Falls down Clark Fork River, Pend Oreille Lake, Priest Lake, and Pend Oreille River nearly to the International Boundary and hunting territories along Salmon River, British Columbia).

(3) The Chewelah (in the country west of the Calispell or Chewelah Mountains in the upper part of the Colville Valley of Washington).

The Lower Kalispel also included several minor bands, the Chewelah apparently two. The Chewelah subdivision spoke a slightly different dialect and was sometimes regarded as an independent tribe.

History: The Kalispel were visited by Lewis and Clark in 1805. In 1809 a post was established on Pend Oreille Lake by the Northwest Company and another on Clark Fork River the same year called Salish House. Emissaries of the American Fur Company reached them later. Roman Catholic priests started working with the Kalispel in 1844 and they were attracted to the priests by the black robes the priests wore and the mystic rituals of that persuasion.

On July 16, 1855, the Upper Kalispel, Kutenai and Salish gave up their lands except for an area at Flathead lake which became the Jocko Reservation. The greater part of the tribe settled there except some of the Lower Kalispel. These Indians went to the Spokane Reservation along with Okanogan, Colville and some other tribes.

Population:

1780	1,200 (Mooney, 1928)
1805	1,600 (Lewis and Clark, 1805-06)
1905	640 Upper Tribe—Jocko Reservation
	197 Lower Tribe—Jocko Reservation
	98 Colville Reservation
1910	386 Montana (U.S. Census)
	158 Washington (U.S. Census)
	15 Idaho (U.S. Census)
	6 other states (U.S. Census)
1930	97 (total)
1965	"about 50" (Editor's interview at Kalispel Reservation, Cusick, Wash.)

1985   259 (total—location not stated)
1987   (See Appendix)

Names by which remembered: City of Kalispell, Montana; Calispell Lake and Mountains. Pend Oreille is remembered by name of Pend Oreille Lake in northern Idaho; river in Montana, Idaho and Washington; county and state park in Washington.

Kutenai

"Tunaha," "Kitunahan," "Kootenay"
Wayne Suttles, writing for the Oregon Historical Society in 1985 states "Kootenay isolate, no recognized phylum." Yenne states: "Algonquian".
Also called:

> Flatbows, the name given often to the Lower Kutenai, the origin is unknown.
> Kúspelu, Nez Percé name, signifying "water people."
> Sán'ka or asán'ka, own name, significance unknown.
> Shalsa'ulk, by the Sinkiuse, said to be from a place name.
> Skelsá-ulk, Salish name, signifying "Water People."
> Slender Bows, name sometimes given as an interpretation of their own name.

Location: Along the upper Columbia River in Canada, northwestern Montana, the northern edge of Idaho and northeastern Washington. Particulars of the Kutenai are in the literature dealing with Indians of western Canada.

The Kutenai were considerably inconvenienced by the establishment of the 49th parallel as the international border as the their tribal lands extended on both sides of the line. It remains unclear just how many were in the United States or in Canada on any given date. Some conjecture and census records show:
Population:

1780   1,200 (Mooney, 1928)
1890   400-500 estimated in U.S.—states not identified
1905   554 in U.S.—states not identified
1910   538 in U.S.—states not identified

Indians Along the Oregon Trail

1924   450 in Canada (Canadian Dept. of Indian Affairs)
        129 in U.S. (Swanton states this number is "defective")
1930   287 (185 Montana; 105 Idaho)
1937   118 in Idaho
1985   123 in Idaho
1987   (See Appendix)

Names by which remembered: Kootenay (Kootenai) River, lake; mountains; falls; county, city of Kootenai in Idaho.

Nez Perce
"Pierced noses" (French)
Also called:

> A'dal-k'ato'igo, Kiowa name, ("people with hair cut across the forehead")
> Aníörspi, Calapooya name
> A-pa-o-pa, Atsina name
> A-pu-pe', Crow name, ("to paddle," "paddles")
> Blue Muds, name applied by traders
> Chopunnish, Lewis and Clark
> Green Wood Indians, Henry-Thompson Journal
> I'-na-cpe, Quapaw name
> Kamu'inu, own name
> Ko-mun'-i-tup'-i-o, Siksika name
> Mikadeshitchísi, Kiowa Apache name
> Nimipu, own name, ("the people")
> Pa ka'-san-tse, Osage name ("plaited hair over the forehead")
> Pe ga'-zan-de, Kansa name
> Pierced Noses, French translation
> Po'-ge-hdo-ke, Dakota name
> Sa-áptin, Okanagon name
> Shi'wanish, Tenino name for this tribe and the Cayuse, ("strangers from up the river")
> Tchaχsúkush, Caddo name
> Thoig'a-rik-kah, Shoshoni name, ("louse eaters(?)")
> Tsuhárukats, Pawnee name
> Tsútpeli, own name

Linguistic group: Shapwailutan, Shahaptian division
Location: Occupation of most of central Idaho and nearby areas of northeast Oregon and southwest Washington.

Idaho

Subdivisions identified by Spinden in 1908:

Alpowe'ma, on Alpaha (Alpowa) Creek (west of Clarkston, Wash.)

Atskaaiwawixpu, at the mouth of the northern fork of Clearwater River

Esnime, Slate Creek Band, the Upper Salmon River Indians

Hasotino, at Hasutin, opposite Asotin, Wash.

Hatwёme, on Hatweh Creek

Heswéiwewipu, at the mouth of Asotin Creek at Snake River

Hinsepu, at Hansen's Ferry on the Grande Ronde River

Imnáma, on Imnaha River

Inantoínu, at the mouth of Joseph Creek

Isäwisnemepu, near Zindels, on the Grande Ronde River

Iwatöinu, at Kendrick on Potlatch Creek

Kamiaxpu, at Kamiah, at the mouth of Lawyer's Creek; this band also called Uyame

Lamtáma, on Salmon River

Lapweme, on Lapwai and Sweetwater Creeks

Makapu, on Cottonwood or Maka Creek

Painíma, near Peck, on Clearwater River

Pipu'inímu, on Big Cañon Creek

Saiksaikinpu, on the upper portion of the Southern Fork of Clearwater River

Sakánma, between the mouth of the Salmon River and the mouth of the Grande Ronde River

Sálwepu, on the Middle Fork of Clearwater River, about five miles above Kooskia

Saxsano, about four miles above Asotin, Wash., on the east side of Snake River

Simínekempu, at Lewiston

Taksehepu, at Agatha on Clearwater River

Tamanmu, at the mouth of Salmon River

Tewepu, at the mouth of Orofino Creek

Toiknimapu, above Joseph Creek on the north side of the Grande Ronde River

Tsokolaikiinma, between Lewiston and Alpowa Creek

Tuke'liklikespu, at Big Eddy

Tukpäme, on the lower portion of the South Fork of Clearwater River

Tunèhepu, at Juliaetta on Potlatch Creek

Walwáma, in Willowa Valley

Wewi'me, at the mouth of the Grande Ronde river

Witkispu, about three miles below Alpowa Creek, on the south side of Snake River

Yakto'inu, at the mouth of Potlach Creek

Yatóinu, on Pike Creek

The Nuksiwepu, Sahatpu, Wawawipu, Almotipu, Pin-ewewewixpu, Tokalatoinu, and other bands extended about 80 miles down Snake River from Lewiston in the vicinity of Lower Monumental Dam.

History: Lewis and Clark marched through the Nez Perce country on their way west in 1805 and again on their return east the next year. A few years later other overland hikers, the Wilson Price Hunt expedition, passed throught (1810). The Rev. Henry Harmon Spaulding, and his wife Eliza Hart Spaulding, founded the Presbyterian Lapwai Mission in 1836 and brought the first printing press to Idaho. Among other items, they printed a hymnal for the Indians.

Rambunctious white miners, often well fortified with liquor, encroached on the Nez Perce to a considerable extent after gold was discovered in the Orofino area in the early 1860s. The thrust of miners, followed by freight wagons, paid no concern for trespass through lands the Indians considered theirs.

Although a reservation had been established at Lapwai, about ten miles up the Clearwater River from Lewiston, the Nez Perce had no intention of being hemmed by rules of the government and a fence. Their refusal to accept reservation life was the cause of the Nez Perce Indian War of 1877. Under the leadership of young Chief Joseph, the Nez Perce outwitted and embarrassed the army, which was forced to bring in a General Officer for its command. Books dealing with the Nez Perce War are numerous, thus this summary will suffice.

In most cases the Government has been successful in persuading Indians to give up their lands and go to reservations which had been established as rapidly as possible. But the authorities were annoyed because they had been unable to persuade the nontreaty Nez Perces to accept the treaty of 1863 and move to the Lapwai Reservation.

The reservation had been a bone of contention for many years. Old Chief Joseph died in 1872 but before his death he received a pledge from his son, Joseph, who was the new chief, never to give up the Wallowa Valley in

Oregon. The government agreed and ceded the valley back to the Indians in 1873. But the federal government demanded it back two years later. Joseph was furious and had a hard time controlling quite a band of hot-headed warriors.

In 1877 a final attempt was made to force the Nez Perces in the Wallowas to move to the Lapwai Reservation in Idaho, surrendering rights to the valley of the Wallowa. A three-day council was called at Lapwai but disagreements culminated in the arrest of the Indians' holy man. He had firmly announced that he would not go on the new reservation. Although the enraged Indians demanded immediate war, Chief Joseph was able to contain their wrath with an agreement to go to Lapwai within a month.

Back in the Wallowa Valley, disgruntled Indians continued to talk with Chief Joseph about their utter unwillingness to accept life on a reservation. With no other course open to them, they believed, the Nez Perce warriors led by their chief, pounced upon unsuspecting settlers around the mouth of the Salmon River and began to exterminate all whites they came across. This slaughter was so great that the army at Fort Lapwai dispatched two companies of cavalry to break up the fighting and escort the remaining Indians to the reservation. In what has become known as the Battle of White Bird, Chief Joseph's warriors nearly wiped out one of the cavalry units and so defeated the other that Captain Perry, the field commander, was forced to retreat. This was on June 17, 1877. Drivers along Highway 95 today will see the Safety Rest Area and Interpretative Center of the Nez Perce National Historic Park—White Bird Battlefield Area, a few miles north of the town of White Bird.

General O. O. Howard put together a punitive force of 600 troops and set out to put down the Nez Perce. In the meantime, Joseph brought all his warriors and their families together and announced they would work their way as peacefully as possible to Canada—out of reach of the federal government. General Howard overtook the slowly moving Indians near Kamiah on the Clearwater River where he engaged the Indians in a two-day battle. The army was able to dislodge the Indians but losses were heavy on both sides.

Chief Joseph led his band over the Lolo Trail, keeping ahead of the troops. The Indians were burdened with all their possessions and the children as well as their infirm, while the army was burdened with the usual impediments of travel due to the very nature of military movements of the period—cumbersome equipment and only one speed: slow. Joseph eluded the troops at every turn, crossing the Bitterroot Mountains and the continental divide then over hundreds of miles of prairie.

The frustrated General could catch the Indians by only one means. He telegraphed ahead to have troops of the Seventh Cavalry under Colonel Nelson "Bearcoat" Miles from Fort Keogh intercept.

On August 9 and then on September 13, Chief Joseph out-maneuvered the army's best and escaped each time. Finally, about two days' march ahead of the army, Joseph had to stop to rest his people. He was within about a day's march into Canada. Colonel Miles slipped his best cavalry unit up to Joseph's camp, caused casualties and surrounded the Indians. This was a five-day battle settled apparently only after the army engaged its Hotchkiss automatic-firing five-barrel cannon which pounded the camp. With no escape, and seeing his people dropping around him, Chief Joseph, an eloquent speaker, surrendered. He declared, in part,

> ...I am tired of fighting. Our chiefs are killed...we have no blankets. The little children are freezing to death.... Hear me, my chiefs! I am tired; my heart is sick and sad. From where the sun now stands, I will fight no more forever.

Although Colonel Miles had promised to send the Nez Perce to the Lapwai Reservation, he entrained them to (Oklahoma) Indian Territory. There were 431 survivors of Joseph's party, which had numbered about 500.

Joseph went to Washington D.C. to plead for his

people. In 1885 the 280 remaining were returned to Lapwai except for Joseph, who was sent to Spokane Reservation northwest of Spokane, Washington. He died there on September 21, 1904.

Population:

1780	4,000 (Mooney, 1928)
1805	6,000 (Lewis and Clark—known too large)
1849	3,000 (Wilkes)
1853	1,700 (Gibbs)
1885	1,437 (B.I.A.)
1906	1,534 Lapwai Reservation
	83 Colville Reservation
1910	1,259 (1,035 Lapwai; 224 Colville—U.S. Census)
1923	1,415 (B.I.A.)
1937	1.426 (B.I.A.)
1950	1,400 (Yenne)
1970	2,251 (Yenne)
1985	2,015 Lapwai (now Nez Perce) Reservation
1987	(See Appendix)

Names by which remembered: Nez Perce county, city in Lewis County, Idaho. Nez Perce Indian Reservation.

Paiute (Northern)

Some of these Indians from Nevada entered Idaho on the southeast corner for hunting from time to time.

Palouse

Although its main area was in Washington, bands of the Palouse entered Idaho along the Palouse River on hunting expeditions. (See Washington)

Salish

"Flathead"

Salish Indians came into Idaho from Montana, but their trips seemed of a temporary nature. (See Montana)

Shoshoni, Northern

Also called:

Aliatan, a name taken originally from the Ute and
subsequently applied to many Shoshoni tribes,
including the Shoshoni proper
Bik-ta'-she, Crow name, ("grass lodges")
E-wu-h'a'-wu-si, Arapaho name, ("people that use
grass or bark for their houses or huts")
Gens du Serpent, by the French
Ginebigônini, Chippewa name, ("snake men")
Kinebikowininiwak, Algonkin name, ("serpents")
Ma-buc-sho-roch-pan-ga, Hidatsa name
Miká-atí, Hidatsa name, ("grass lodges")
Mi'kyashe, Crow name, ("grass lodges")
Pezhi'-wokeyotila, Teton Dakota name, ("grass
thatch dwellers")
Pi-ci'-kse-ni-tup'i-o, Siksika name
Sin-te'-hda wi-ca-sa, Yankton Dakota name, ("rattlesnake
Indians")
Sisízhanin, Atsina name, ("rattlesnake men")
Snake Indians, common English name
Snóa, Okanagon name
Wákidoħka-numak, Mandan name, ("snake man")
Wes'anikaci-ga, Omaha and Ponca name, ("snake
people")
Zuzéca wićása, Teton Dakota name, ("snake people")

Linguistic group: Uto-Aztecan, Shoshoni-Ccomanche
dialect Shoshonean division.

Location: The Northern Shoshoni occupied eastern
Idaho, except the territory held by the Bannock; western
Wyoming; and northeastern Utah.

Subdivisions: The only known subdivisions were a few
bands led by local chiefs, the makeup of these groups
continually changing. So-called permanent villages were:

Lemhi and Central Idaho:
Bohodai, near the junction of Middle Fork with the Salmon,
and an unnamed site on upper Salmon River where a few
families from Sohodai sometimes wintered.
Guembeduka, about 7 miles north of the town of Salmon.
Padai, scattered along Lemhi River about Salmon.
Pagadut, on Red Rock Creek, about Lima, Montana; possibly a
few families lived near Dillon, Montana.
Pasasigwana, at a warm spring in the mountains north of
Clayton.

Pasimadai, on Upper Salmon River.
Sohodai, on the upper Middle Fork of Salmon River, near Three
Rivers.
Fort Hall Shoshoni: No band names given.
Bannock Creek (Kamduka) Shoshoni (Pocatello's Band):
    Biagamugep, the principal village, near Kelton.
Cache Valley (Pangwiduka) Kwagunogwai:
    Along the Logan River above its junction with the Little Bear
    River.
Salt Lake Valley:
    There are said to have been bands in the Ogden, Weber, and Salt
    Lake Valleys, but their names have not been preserved.

History: The Shoshoni inhabited the Great Basin from
southern Colorado to eastern Oregon and shared the area
with the Paiute, Ute, Bannock and Gosiute with a
relationship that included inter-tribal marriage. The Shoshoni were plausibly the closest to Stone Age culture than
other tribes from a technological standpoint. Rather than
hunting with bow and arrow, or even spears, these Indians
hid behind brush and struck rabbits and other small game
with clubs.

At one time the Northern Shoshoni extended farther
eastward into the plains, yet there is no reason to assume
they did not, at the same time, retain mountain territories
later used.

The Shoshoni were affected only indirectly by the
Spanish settlements to the south and southwest. The
Shoshoni were pleased as well as amazed to see one of their
own, the teen-aged Indian girl, Sacajawea, leading a
procession of strangers (Lewis and Clark) onto their land in
1805. From this time on contact with Americans was fairly
common and friendly, probably because of their first
encounter with the Lewis and Clark Expedition. The
Northern Shoshoni, especially those under the influence of
the famous Chief Washakie, seemed to go out of their way
to be friendly. They were finally gathered upon the Lemhi
and Fort Hall Reservations in Idaho and the Wind River
Reservation in Wyoming. By the Treaty of Fort Bridger,
July 3, 1868, the eastern bands of the Shoshoni and
Bannock ceded all rights to their territories in Wyoming and

Idaho, except the Wind River Reservation in Wyoming for the Shoshoni, and a reservation to be set apart for the Bannock whenever they wanted it.

On July 30, 1869, Fort Hall Reservation was reserved for the Bannock but later jointly occupied by the Shoshoni. February 12, 1875, the Lemhi Reservation was established for these two tribes and the Sheepeater band of Western Shoshoni.

Because of his great friendship with the whites and influence over his people, Chief Washakie was made an Honorary Captain in the Army. Accordingly, when he died in 1900, he was accorded a full military funeral by the U.S. Government. Chief Washakie is undoubtedly the only Indian so honored.

Population:

1845	4,500 (includes Western Shoshoni—Mooney, 1928)
1910	3,840 (about 2,000 Northern; 1,840 Western—U.S. Census)
1917	2,200 (B.I.A.)
1930	3,994 (about 1,190 Northern; 2,0884 Western—U.S. Census)
1937	2,600 (about 2,400 Northern; 1,201 Western—B.I.A.)
1985	1,236 (in Nevada reservations)
	? (unstated but known in Idaho)
1987	(See Appendix)

Names by which remembered: The name "Shoshoni" was chosen as the name of linguistic group now considered part of a larger group, the Uto-Aztecan. The name became popular because the Indian girl Sacajawea (pron: Sah-cah-ga-we-ah) also called "Bird Woman," acted as guide and interpreter for Lewis and Clark, thus paving the way for friendliness between the Shoshoni and the whites. Shoshoni Chief Washakie was a constant friend of the whites. Also a name for mountains and rivers in Wyoming and Nevada, a lake in Yellowstone National Park, a falls in the Snake River in Idaho, a county in Idaho, and towns in California, Idaho, Nevada and Wyoming.

Shoshoni, Western

Location: Western Shoshoni ranged from south-central and western Idaho and the corner of northwestern Utah, northeastern and central deserts of Nevada to southeast California in the vicinity of Death and Panamint Valleys.

Subdivisions: The names of many local groups have been recorded, usually indicating they were "eaters" of certain foods, but most of these seem to have belonged to territories rather than people, the "eaters" in each being subject to change. A few, however, acquired special interest or any measure of permanence as the Tukuarike, Tukudaduka, or Sheep Eaters, extending from Yellowstone National Park to the middle course of the Salmon River; the Gosiute of northern Utah and eastern Nevada and the Panamint or Koso, the Californian representatives of the division.

Villages: The Western Shoshoni inhabited such an extreme area that the numbers of villages seem well over 200. The majority of these appear to be in California, Colorado, Nevada.

History: The two Shoshoni, Northern and Western, have almost the same history except that the general area of the Western Shoshoni was away from the routes traveled by the pioneers on their way west (Nebraska, Wyoming, Idaho, Oregon) and north of the routes of the Spanish, and others, through Arizona and New Mexico.

In 1825 Jedidiah Smith made several journeys across Nevada and may have been preceded by Old Greenwood. In 1847 the Mormons settled Nevada and came in contact with some of the eastern bands. Narratives of explorers generally waste few words on these Indians or the neighboring Paiute, classing them indiscriminately as "diggers" and calling them vile words. The Indians were affected materially by the discovery of the Comstock Lode. Although the mining areas were not in their territory, prospectors penetrated everywhere. Stock was brought in which sorely affected the food supplies of the natives. The resulting friction affected first the Northern Paiute and somewhat later the Shoshoni.

Population: See chart for Northern Shoshoni.

Names by which remembered: See Northern Shoshoni.

Skitswish
Also called:

> Coeur d'Alêne, a French appellation meaning "awl
> heart," siad to have been used originally by a
> chief to indicate the size of a trader's heart
> Q'ma'shpal, Yakima name, ("camas people")
> Pointed Hearts, from the word Coeur d'Alêne
> Ski-zoo-mish, as frequently written
> Skeet-so-mish, as called by Lewis and Clark

Linguistic group: Salishan, inland division being closest to Kalispels

Location: Around Lake Coeur d'Alene, its tributaries and the Spokane River as far west as Spokane Falls (City of Spokane). Some bands lived as far southeast as the upper stretches of the Clearwater River.

Subdivisions and villages: Teit (1930) reports divisions and villages, noting that the last may have included two sections, the Coeur d'Alêne Lake Division and the Spokane River Division.

St. Joe River Division:
> Ntcaamtsen (.ntcäa'mtsɛn), at the confluence of the St. Joe and St. Maries Rivers.
> Stiktakeshen (.sti'qᵘtakɛcɛn?), near the mouth of St. Joe River, on the river, or nearby on the lake.
> Stotseawes (stotsɛäwɛs), St. Joe River, at the place now called Fish Trap.
> Takolks (ta'x.olks) (?), at headwaters (spring) of Hangman's Creek near base of hill just south of De Smet.
> Tcatowashalgs (tcat'owacalgs), on St. Joe River a little above Stotseawes.
> Tcetishtasheshen (tcêti'ctacɛcɛn), Probably on the lake, near the Stiktakeshen, on the north or east side, not far from the mouth of the river.
Coeur d'Alêne River Division:
> Athlkwarit (alqwarit), at Harrison.
> Gwalit (gwa'lît), near the lake and close to Harrison.
> Hinsalut (hînsä'lut), on Coeur d'Alêne River a little above Smakegen.

Kokolshtelps (qoqolc'têlps), a little above Nestagwast.

Nalstkathlkwen (nalstqa'l χwεn), a little above Senshalemants.

Neatskstem (ne'atsxstεm), on Coeur d'Alêne River a little above Athlkwarit.

Nêstagwast (nest'a'gwast), at Black Lake, at a tributary river and lake here.

Senshalemants (sεncä'lεmänts), a little above Hinsalut.

Smakegen (sma'qεgen), at Medimont. Skwato (sk'wat'o'), at old mission.

Tclatcalk (tcla'tcalxw), on Coeur d'Alêne Lake near the mouth of Coeur d'Alêne River.

Coeur d'Alêne Lake and Spokane River Division:

Ntaken (nt'a'q'εn), Hayden Lake, north of Coeur d'Alêne Lake.

Tcelatcelitcemen (tcêlätcelîtcεmεn), halfway around Coeur d'Alêne Lake on the east side.

Ntcemkainkwa (ntc'εmqa'inqwa), at Coeur d'Alêne.

Smethlethlena (smεiεie'na), near the last on the same side.

Tpoenethlpem, very near the preceding, on the same side.

Nsharept (nca'rεpt), a little below the next to the last.

Stcatkwei (stcatkwe'i), a little below the last.

Kamilen (q'ämi'len), at Post Falls.

Hinsaketpens (hinsaq'a'tpεns), about one mile above the Spokane bridge (*The phrase "one mile above the Spokane bridge" is unclear. Is Swanton, who wrote it, referring to a bridge across the Spokane River at the city of Spokane, or is he looking at the town of Spokane Bridge? This town was on the river but 16 miles east of the city of Spokane and about 5½ miles west of Post Falls, Idaho. —Editor*).

Newashalks (ne'εwa'calqs), a little below the preceding. Ntset-sawolsako (ntsetsakwolsa'ko?), on Tamarack Creek, toward the mountains in Clearwater County, Idaho.

Neshwahwe (nesxwa'xxwe), on the river a little below the last two.

Nesthlihum (nesli'xum), a little below the last.

Tcanokwaken (tcanokwa'kεn?), a little below the last.

Mulsh (mu'lc), at Green Acres.

Tcatenwahetpem (tcatenwa'xetpεm), a short distance below Green Acres, and about 20 miles above Spokane City.

History: There is no evidence of migrations of the Skitswish tribe and apparently the tribe was unknown until brought to the attention of Lewis and Clark.

This tribe was almost never known to be war-like or unfriendly. Although there was a strong protest by the

Indians about white encroachment in 1858, this uprising was quickly put down. The Skitswish were quite docile, nevertheless they were self-respecting and industrious. Early French travelers (*voyageurs*) gave them the name "Coeur d'Alene" and told of them "having spirits that were small and hard...particularly shrewd in trade." As was true with many tribes, these Indians had no immunity to white man's diseases, thus this tribe suffered heavily. As settlers took over the tribal areas, particularly west of Lake Coeur d'Alene, establishing towns and huge agricultural tracts (as Otis Orchards), along and near the Spokane River—including an electric train that ran back-and-forth between Spokane and Coeur d'Alene—these Indians were eventually contained on a reservation.

Population:

1780	1,000 (Mooney, 1928)
1800	between 3,000-4,000 (Teit, 1930)
1905	494 (B.I.A.)
1910	293 (U.S. Census)
	601 (B.I.A., probably includes Spokane)
1937	608 (B.I.A.)
1987	(See Appendix)

Names by which remembered: Skitswish: peak (4,900 ft. elev.); creek. Coeur d'Alene: city; lake, river, mountain; national forest; valley.

Snakes (See Paiute, Northern)

Spokan (See Washington)

Great Northern train No. 10 entering Coeur d'Alene yard from Spokane.

—Photo courtesy of Clyde Parent

CHAPTER 4

OREGON

Ahantchuyuk
Significance of name undetermined.
Also called:

French Prairie Indians, by early settlers in Marion County.
Pudding River Indians

Linguistic group: Kalapooian
Tribal land was along or near the Pudding River in the
Willamette Valley.
No population statistics available.

Alsea
The name is from Alsi, their own name of unknown
meaning.
Also called:

Kûnis'tûnne, Chastacosta name.
Päifan amím, Luckiamute Kalapuya name.
Si ni'-te-li tunne, Naltunne name, meaning "flatheads."
Tcha yá χo amim, Luckiamute Kalapuya name.
Tehayesátlu, Nestucca name.
Ulseah, by Lewis and Clark.

Linguistic group: Yakonan
Location: On Oregon coast at Alsea Bay (Waldport)
and on Alsea River.
Villages:

Chiink, on the south side of Alsea River.
Kakhtshanwaish, on north side of Alsea River.
Kalbusht, on the lower course of Alsea River.
Kauhuk, on the south side of Alsea River.
Kaukhwan, on the north side of Alsea River at Beaver Creek.
Khlimkwaish, on the south side of Alsea River.
Khlokhwaiyutslu, on the north side of Alsea River.

Kutauwa, on the north side of Alsea River at its mouth.
Kwamk, on the south side of Alsea River.
Kwulisit, on the south side of Alsea River.
Kyamaisu, on the north side of Alsea River at its mouth.
Panit, on the south side of Alsea River.
Shiuwauk, on the north side of Alsea River.
Skhakhwaiyutslu, on the south side of Alsea River.
Tachuwit, on the north side of Alsea River.
Thlekuhweyuk, on the south side of Alsea River.
Thlekushauk, on the south side of Alsea River.

The Alsea occupied small tracts near the mouth of Alsea River, but little is known of their early history. Corning wrote that these Indians apparently existed in quite some numbers in the 1840-50 period; they had nearly all expired by the 1890 count.
Population:

1890   12 (Siletz Reservation)
1910   29 (U.S. Census)
1930   9 (entire Yakonan group, U.S. Census)

Names by which remembered: Alsea bay, town (ZIP 97324), river.

Atfalati
"'Fallatahs'" (meaning unknown); "Tualati" (Tualatin)
Also called:

Wapato Lake Indians, name used by early travelers.

Linguistic group: Kalapooian, northern dialect.
Location: In the hills around Forest Grove near village of Wapato, near present Gaston, and on Wapato Lake, a "lake" in very wet years—an intermittent lake. Remnants of the Atfalati were sent to Grande Ronde Reservation. Little is known of their customs.
Villages:

Chachambitmanchal, 3½ miles north of Forest Grove.
Chachamewa, at Forest Grove, 6 miles from Wapato Lake.

Chachanim, on Wapato Lake prairie.

Chachif, on Wapato Lake.

Chachimahiyuk, between Wapato Lake and Willamette River, Washington County.

Chachimewa, on or near Wapato Lake, Yamhill County.

Chachokwith, at a place of the same name north of Forest Grove, Washington County.

Chagindueftei, between Hillsboro and Sauvies Island, Washington County.

Chahelim, in Chehelim Valley, 5 miles south of Wapato Lake, Yamhill County.

Chakeipi, about 10 miles west of Oregon City.

Chakutpaliu, northeast of Hillsboro, Washington County.

Chalal, near the outlet of Wapato Lake.

Chalawai, southeast of Wapato Lake.

Chamampit, on Wapato Creek at the east end of Wapato Lake.

Chapanaghtin, north of Hillsboro, Washington County.

Chapokele, 4 miles west of Wapato Lake.

Chapungathpi, at Forest Grove, Washington County.

Chatagihl, at the upper end of Wapato Lake.

Chatagithl, at the upper end of Wapato Lake.

Chatagshish, in Washington County.

Chatakuin, 7 miles north of Hillsboro, Washington County.

Chatamnei, 10 miles north of Wapato Lake, in Washington County.

Chatilkuei, 5 miles west of Wapato Lake, in Yamhill County.

Chawayed, west of Forest Grove, in Washington County.

Population:

1860ca.	20 (Grande Ronde Reservation)
1910	44 (U.S. Census)

Names by which remembered: Tualatin (ZIP 97062).

Bannock

Bannock entered Oregon from Idaho in the area between the confluences of the Snake River with the Powder and Owyhee Rivers. The city of Weiser, Idaho, is in about the center of this area. (See Idaho)

Calapooya (Kalapuya)
Also called:

Calla-puya, by Wilkes
Collapoewah, by Lewis and Clark
Calapooa, by Parker
Calapooyas, by Lee and Frost
Kaita-ka, by the Umpquas
Tsanh-alokual amin, by Luckimute Kalapuya

Linguistic group: The name, properly speaking, of a division of the Kalapooian family formerly occupying the watershed between Willamette and Umpqua rivers. The term as usually employed, however, includes all the bands speaking dialects of the Kalapooian language and is made synonymous with the family name. This double use of the term, coupled with the scanty information regarding the division, brings confusion in the classification of the bands which apparently cannot be rectified.

Location: In the mountains on headwaters of McKenzie and Willamette Rivers.

Subdivisions:

Amphishtna, east of upper Willamette River.
Tsanchifin, on the site of Eugene City.
Tsanklighemifa, at Eugene City.
Tsankupi, at Brownsville, Linn County.
Tsawokot, north of Eugene City.

Population:

1780	3,000 (all Kalapooian—Mooney, 1928)
1880	351 (Grande Ronde Reservation)
1890	164 (Grande Ronde Reservation)
1905	130 (Grande Ronde Reservation)
1910	5 Calapooya (106 entire stock—U.S. Census)
1930	0 Calapooya (45 entire stock—U.S. Census)

Names by which remembered: Tribal name used for all tribes of the stock. Calapooya River, creek, mountains.

Cascade (See Watlala)

Cayuse
Also called:

Caaguas	Kinse
Cailoux	Kiosse
Cajouses	Kiuses
Cayouses	Kiwaw
Cayus	Kay-use
Conguses	Kayoose
Cyuse	Rayouse
Hal'luntchi	Skiuses
Kagouse	Skyness
Kayouse	Waiiletpu
Kayul	Wailetpu (own name)
Kayuxes	Waillatpus
Keyuses	Waulapta
Kieoux	Yeletpo

Linguistic group: Shapwailutan.

Location: In headwaters of Walla Walla, Umatilla and Grande Ronde Rivers and from the Blue Mountains as far as Deschutes River in Washington and Oregon.

History: Noted by Lewis and Clark in 1805. Closely associated with the Nez Perce and Walla Walla tribes; so closely that inter-marriages eventually wiped out their own dialect. Cayuse were well known to pioneers, fur trappers and settlers. The name Cayuse is usually associated with that of the Whitman Mission which was established by Dr. Marcus and his wife Narcissa Prentice Whitman at Waiila-tpu ("place of the rye-grass") in 1836 seven miles west of the city of Walla Walla. On November 29, 1847, following a severe smallpox epidemic, which the doctor was unable to stop, the doctor, his wife, and others were murdered in what is recorded as the "Whitman Massacre." (Whitman Mission National Historic Site, National Park Service)

It was the misfortune of the Cayuse to live astride a major immigration trail over which pioneers poured on their way to the Willamette Valley. Many of these emigrants, destitute after the long walk from the middle west, sought refuge with the Whitmans, no doubt giving the Cayuse a reason to think they were being pushed from their land.

By 1851 the Cayuse were so greatly reduced in numbers they partially merged with the Nez Perce. Two years later they joined in a treaty that formed the Umatilla Reservation.

Population:

1780	500 (Mooney, 1928)
1904	404
1910	298 (U.S. Census)
1923	337 (B.I.A.)
1930	199 (combined with Molalla)
1937	370 (Cayuse only—B.I.A.)
1987	(See Appendix)

Reasons and names by which remembered: The Cayuse earned a reputation of plausibly being the most warlike tribe in Washington and Oregon. It was members of this tribe who murdered Dr. and Mrs. Whitman and eleven others at the mission. The Cayuse were experts with horse breeding, thus the term "cayuse" became the word used to describe a horse, especially a young, strong, fast Indian pony. There is an Oregon town (ZIP 97821); a canyon.

Chastacosta

"Shas-te-koos-tee," "Shista-kwusta" (their own name)
Also called:

Atchásliti ame'nmei, by the Atfalati Kalapuya.
Atchashti ámim, another form of the Kalapuya name.
Katuku, by the Shasta.
Shastacosta, by whites.
Wálamskni, by the Klamath.
Wálamswash, by the Modoc.

Linguistic group: Athapascan
Location: Mostly along north bank of Rogue River from confluence with Illinois River upstream to convergence of Rogue and Applegate Rivers. (Takilma Indians [which see] were near-neighbors on the south side of Rogue River.)
Villages:

Chetuttunne.
Chunarghuttunne, east of the junction of Rogue River and
    Applegate River.
Chunsetunneta.
Chunsetunnetun.

Chushtarghasuttun.
Chusterghutmunnetun, the highest on Rogue River.
Chuttushshunche.
Khloshlekhwuche.
Khotitachecche.
Khtalutlitunne.
Kthelutlitunne, at the junction of Rogue River and
    a southern affluent.
Kushlatata.
Mekichuntun.
Musme.
Natkhwunche.
Nishtuwekulsushtun.
Sechukhtun.
Senestun.
Setaaye.
Setsurgheake.
Silkhkemechetatun.
Sinarghutlitun.
Skurgnut.
Sukechunetunne.
Surghustesthitun.
Tachikhwutme, above the mouth of Illinois River.
Takasichekhwut.
Talsunme.
Tatsunye.
Thethlkhuttunne.
Tisattunne.
Tsetaame, east of the junction of Rogue River with
    Applegate River.
Tsetutkhlalenitun.
Tukulittatun.
Tukwilisitunne.
Tuslatunne.

History: The Chastacosta were involved with the Rogue
River Indian Wars. In summer 1856, after several months of
severe fighting against the whites, all of the Indians that
could be found, numbering 156 (53 men, 61 women, 23
boys, 16 girls) were taken to the Siletz Reservation on the
north Oregon coast. Hodge states, "It is particularly certain
that nearly all the inhabitants of [the] villages were removed
at this time." Considering the number of villages the count
of the inhabitants seems particularly small. There is no

doubt that these Indians did not take well to the foggy and rainy Oregon coast weather considering their home villages were well inland, in the Rogue River canyon—now the Wild and Scenic protected canyon with roaring rapids—where summer temperatures are seldom under 100⁰ F. and there is no rain for months at a time.

Population:

1854	145 (Hodge)
1856	156 (Siletz Reservation)
1905	"a few" (Hodge)
1910	7 (U.S. Census)
1937	30 (B.I.A.)

Names by which remembered: Shasta Costa Creek.

Chelamela

Also called: Long Tom Creek Indians, Lung-tum-ler.

Linguistic group: Calapooian, Calapooya dialect

Location: Along Long Tom River, which appears to be a corruption of the Indian name "Lung-tum-ler."

Population: Apparently none recorded.

Names by which remembered: A river.

Chepenafa

Also called:

Api'nefu, or Pineifu, by the other Kalapuya.
Marys River Indians, the official and popular name.

Linguistic group: Kalapooian, Calapooya dialect

Location: At forks of Mary's River (Benton County) not far from Corvallis. In some references the river is referred to as "St. Marys Creek." McArthur, in *Oregon Geographic Names,* "suggests" the name may have come from early-day French Canadians working for Hudson's Bay Company.

Population:

1910 24 (U.S. Census)

Chetco

("Close-to-the-mouth-of-the-stream")
Linguistic group: Athapascan
Location: Each side of the Chetco River at its mouth with the Pacific Ocean (at present city of Brookings), also along Winchuck River at California border, but specifically, apparently, on the Oregon side although some Chetcos probably were in California long before the border was set in 1848.
   Villages:

Along the Chetco River:
   Chettanne, Khuniliikhwut, Nukhsuchutun, Setthatun, Siskhaslitun, and Tachukhaslitun, on the south side of Chetco River.
   Chettannene, on the north side of Chetco River.
   Nakwutthume, on Chetco River above all the other villages.
   Natitene'tun, about where the modern town of Brookings stands.
   Shri'choslintun, on Chetco River a little above the following.
   Tcagitli'tun, on Chetco River at the mouth of the north fork.
   Tcet or Tectko, at the mouth of Chetco River, really a town on each side.
   Thicharghiliitun, on the upper course of a south branch of Chetco River.
   Tume'stun, near Shri'choslintun.
   Drucker adds that "the coast town which Parrish calls Wishtenatan (Water man, xustene'ten) may have been affiliated more closely with Chetco River than with the Lower Rogue River group."

Along the Winchuck River:
   Hosa'tun, at the mouth of Winchuck River.

There is evidence, based on the nature of the landform, this village was in all probability in the grove of trees just north of the mouth of the river in the area presently occupied by a private trailer park. This region often enjoys Oregon's warmest winter temperatures now known to be partially protected by the along-shore Davidson Current flowing from Baja.
   History: Chetco Indians appeared to have a rather

peaceful existence until the discovery of gold along the southern Oregon coast in 1852. Incoming seekers cared little for the Indians and shoved them aside. These Indians were removed to the Siletz Reservation in 1853 after the whites destroyed the Indian dwellings, some 42 houses.

Population:

    1854   241 (117 men, 83 women, 41 children—
                    Siletz Reservation
    1861   262 (Siletz Reservation)
    1877   63 (Siletz Reservation)
    1910   9 (U.S. Census)

Names by which remembered: A river, a post office 1863-1910), a mountain.

Chetleschantunne

Meaning, "people-among-the-big-rocks."

Location: About the Pistol River and the coast from headlands about 13 miles south of Rogue River. Villages were at Mack's Arch (now Mack Arch) from which they took thier name. Another village at Crook Point (42° 15' N.).

> Villages: Pistol River, on north bank: Mack's Arch (now Mack Arch), Crook Point.

Population:

    1854   51 (Hodge)

Clackamas (Guithlakimas)

Also called:

> Clackamus, by Lewis and Clark.
> Klackamus, by Wilkes.
> Akimmash, Clackimis, Clackamos, Clackemus, Clackemurs, Klackamat, Thlakeimas, Tlakimish, Akimmash,
> Gita q!emas (by the Clatsop), Nsekau's (or Ns tiwatt) by the Nestucca, Tu'hu tane' by Umpqua.

Linguistic group: Chinookian

Location: Along the Clackamas River and along the

east side of the Willamette River about to Oregon City then up the Clackamas River to the mountains.

History: The lands of this tribe were ceded to the U.S. by treaty of 1855 then shortly the people were sent to the Grande Ronde Reservation.

Population:

```
1780   2,500 (Mooney, 1928)
1806   1,800 (estimate by Lewis and Clark)
1851      88 (Swanton)
1910      40 (U.S. Census)
1937      81 (U.S. Office of Indian Affairs)
```

Names by which remembered: A county, city (ZIP 97015); river; Clackamette Park at confluence of Clackamas and Willamette Rivers.

Clahclellah
Also called:

Watala

Linguistic group: Chinookian
Location: Occupied a single village of seven houses near base of the Cascades of the Columbia River, as identified by Lewis and Clark in 1806.
Population: Not observed.

Clahnaquah
Linguistic group: Chinookian
Location: On Sauvies Island, in midst of confluence of Willamette and Columbia Rivers as observed by Lewis and Clark in 1906. The tribe occupied four houses.
Population:

```
1806   130 (Hodge)
```

Clatskanie
Also called:

A'latske	Klatskanai
Clack-star	Tlat-skanie

Linguistic group: Salishan

Location and History: At one time the Clatskanie occupied land in Washington State in prairies along the Chehalis River near mouth of Skookumechuck River at Centralia. When small game failed, the tribe wandered southwesterly and eventually crossed the Columbia River and took space in the mountains at the Clatskanie River. Bands of the tribe settled as far south as the Nehalem River but sites of these villages are unknown. The location on the Clatskanie River at the mouth seems to be the best known historic center. One report indicated these Indians collected toll of all who passed their land, going up or down the Columbia.

Population:

1780	1,600 (Mooney, 1928)
1851	8
1910	3 (U.S. Census)

Names by which remembered: Clatskanie creek, river, city (ZIP 97016), also Klatskanie river.

Clatsop (dried salmon)
Linguistic group: Chinookian
Villages:

Ko-na-pee, near port town of Flavel on Columbia River at west cape where Young's bay meets the river.
Ne-ah-coxie, at mouth of that creek.
Ne-ah-keluc, at Point Adams.
Ne-ahk-stowt, near present Hammond.
Ne-co-tat, at present Seaside.
Quatat, at present Seaside.
Tle-las-qua, at Knappa.
Se-co-mee-tsiuc, on Tongue Point.
O-wa-pun-pun, on Smith's Point.
Nee-tul, on Lewis and Clark River slightly upstream from mouth.
Ne-ahk-al-toun-al-the, on west side Young's Bay.

Ski-per-nawin, at mouth of Skipanon Creek.
Ne-hay-ne-hum, short distance upstream on Nechanicom River.
Ne-ahk-li-paltli, near Elk Creek.

History: The Clatsops were able-bodied and fared for themselves. Had many threats from Chief Comcomley (Chinook) and in turn threatened him.

In 1852 a visiting white discovered about an acre of ground covered with human bones, including skulls, as well as decaying canoes. This plot was a little south of Seaside and was a Clatsop burial ground. A story in the *Morning Oregonian* on October 23, 1899, discussed the burial methods of the Indians who built scaffolds in the trees, about 12 feet above ground at Point Adams in 1854. The body and all the Indian's belongings would be placed here then abandoned. The paper did not mention any correlation between the two burial sites or methods.

There have been many dozens of shipwrecks near the mouth of the Columbia River and often survivors would either be cast ashore in view of the Indians' foraging, or the dead bodies would wash up with the tides. As a result, the Clatsops coined the word "Tlechonnipts" which they defined as "those who drift ashore." In 1875 the tribe was taken to Grande Ronde Reservation.

Population:

1780   300 (Mooney, 1928)
1806   200 (in 14 houses, Lewis and Clark)
1910   26 (U.S. Census)

Names by which remembered: A county; a village near south end of Clatsop Plain (post office 1894-1919); Camp Clatsop, Oregon National Guard summer camp (now Camp Rilea); Fort Clatsop National Memorial; a community college; a spit.

Clowwewalla
Pronounced: Gilay'wee-walamt
Also called:

| Fall Indians | Willamette Indians |
| Tumwater Indians | Willamette Falls Indians. |

Linguistic group: Chinookian
Location: Around the falls of the Willamette River (Oregon City).

Subdivisions: It is presumed this tribe might have included Cushooks, Chahcowahs and Nemalquinner. Lewis and Clark called them Cushooks.

Population:

1780	900 (Mooney, 1928)
1805-06	650 (Lewis and Clark)
1829	13 (reduced by illness)

Coos (see Hanis)

Coquille (see Mishikhwutmetunne)

Cow Creek

Location: Along Cow Creek, Douglas County, since mid-1880s occupied by the creek and the Southern Pacific railroad track in the narrow defile, and on the wide valley floor upstream near today's town of Azalea. (See Umpqua)

History: These Indians are often mentioned by Heckert and are included in Walling.

Dakubetede

Also called: Applegate River Indians; NI'ckite hitclum, the Alsea name ("people far up the stream"); Ts'u-qus-li'qwut-me' tunne.

Linguistic group: Athapascan

Location: On Applegate River.

History: There is some evidence these inhabitants of the Applegate River Valley were in communication with the Chastacosta. The two tribes were of the same language group and the Applegate feeds into the Rogue River in an area known to have been occupied by the Chastacosta.

Population: There seems no count of these Indians, however in Mooney's 1928 study he estimated there were a total of about 3,200 when combined with Nahankhotane, division of Umpquas; Taltushtuntde and the Umpqua.

Dog River (See Watlala)

Hanis (Also called "Hanis Coos")
Linguistic group: Kusan. One of two members, the other being the Miluk.
Location: On Coos River and along the bay.
Villages:

> Anasioth, south side of Coos Bay near Empire
> Melukita, north side of Coos Bay.

History: The Hanis and their neighborly Miluks lived in harmony, fished and hunted together in an area bounded by Lakeside, a community on the east shore of Coos Bay, and to Tenmile Creek, to Whiskey Run on the south. This seemed an area for good living as the forests abounded with deer, elk, bear, even panther and wildcats. There was fish for the taking in the several rivers that emptied into the bay as well as fish and oysters in the bay. There was no shortage of small game along with a great wild crop of various berries—all kept well moistened by the considerable rain and fog of the area as well as brilliant summer days. While camas root as a food has been associated with the inland Indians (see under Bannock—Idaho), this bulb crop was plentiful for the Hanis and Miluks to harvest near Whiskey Run. These Indians also ventured as ar as Camas Valley (southwest of Roseburg) for this crop.

Many of these Indians were tattooed. They also adorned themselves with ear and nose decorations of small seashells or bones. Due to the diversity of the weather any dress they wore was seasonal. Cold-weather clothing was of animal skins and valuable furs.

These tribes died off as the years went by. In the book *A Century of Coos and Curry* [counties] published in 1952, the text suggests there was a Coos woman living at the time in the Empire district of Coos Bay.

Population:

1780 2,000 Hanis and Miluk combined (Mooney, 1928)
1805 1,500 Hanis (Lewis and Clark)
1910 93 (U.S. Census—both tribes)
1930 197 (U.S. Census)
1937 55 (U.S. Office of Indian Affairs)

Names by which remembered: References are under "Coos": Name of a city (ZIP 97420); bay, river; Coos Head, the point on south side of entrance to the bay; a town Cooston (post office 1908-1929).

Klamath
Also called:

Aígspaluma, abbreviated to Aígspalo, Aíspalu; Nez Percé name for all Indians on Klamath Reservation and in vicinity, meaning "people of the chipmunks."
Alámmimakt ísh (from ala'mmig, "Upper Klamath Lake"), said to be the Achomawi name.
Athlámeth, Calapooya name.
Aúksiwash, in Yreka dialect of Shasta.
Clammittes, by Peter Skene Ogden.
Dak'-ts!aªm-al-a or Dak'-ts!a°w-an-a', "those above the lakes," by the Takelma.
E-ukshik-ni máklaks, meaning "people of the lakes," also their own name.
Makaítserk, by the western Shasta.
Plaíkni, collective name for Klamath, Modoc, and Snakes on Sprague River.
Sáyi, Northern Paiute name.
Tapáadji, Ilmawi name.
Wols, name given by the Latgawa.

Linguistic group: Shapwailutan, Lutuamian division.
Location: Upper Klamath Lake, the Klamath Marsh, Sprague and Williamson Rivers.
Subdivisions and villages:

I. a'ukckni (the Klamath marsh—Williamson River group), with the following villages: mu'tcuia'ksi (near the bridge toward the eastern end of Klamath marsh), k'ɛtaiwa's (along the eastern side of the marsh),

74

gupgua'ksi, (east side of Klamath marsh south of last), i'wal (along a southeastern tongue of the marsh), kla'djoksi (ibid.), du'ʻilkut (on the south shore of Klamath marsh), awa'lwaskan (west of preceding), wa'ktale's (on higher ground where Williamson River leaves the marsh), la'laks (ibid.), lobo'kstsoksi (on the bluff on the left bank of the Sprague River at the railroad bridge) called by Gatschet (1891 b) ktaí-tú-pakshi), an unnamed site (on the south side of Sprague River below the dam), k!otewa'ets (about two miles above the dam on the south bank of Sprague River), koma'eksi (on both sides of Sprague River south of Braymill, four miles from Chiloquin), ka'umkan (about six miles above the last), [Yainax] (settlements of some sort near here), hicdic-lue'lukc (west of Gearhart Mountain), bɛukse'was (on the right bank of Willaimson River below the mouth of Sprague River), tkalma'kcda (on the right bank of Williamson River below preceding), k'tai'di (on flat opposite last mentioned), djigia's (below last two on both sides of river), k!o'ltawas (on both banks below preceding but principally on left bank), at'awikc (below last, principally on right bank), ya'ak (right bank below precding), tsa'k'wi (below last, principally on right), wita'mumpsi (on a high bluff on the right bank above an eddy in the sharp bend in the river), goyɛmske'ɛgis or kiɛke'tsus (on right bank below last), wɛla'lksi (on the eastern shore of Agency Lake), lok'o'gut (on the higher land near Agency Lake by a little warm spring), tco'klalumps (overlooks the lake where the Chiloquin road meets the Agency Lake highway), "other towns may have been at ya'mzi, on the western side of Yamsay Mountain, and kokena'oke, Spring Creek, a large northern affluent of Klamath marsh."

II. kowa'cdikni, perhaps part of the first division, occupying: kowa'cdi (on Agency Lake).

III. du'kwakni (on the delta of Williamson River), affiliated most closely with the next division, and including: mo'aksda (on the left bank of Williamson River nearly a mile above the mouth), wickamdi (below the preceding on the right bank), la'wa'lstot (on the point forming the right side of the mouth of Williamson River), moginkunks (on the left bank of Williamson River a quarter of a mile above the mouth), djingus (at a spring on the lake front to the east of the mouth of Williamson River).

IV. gu'mbotkni (on Pelican Bay and the marsh to the north) including: sle'tsksi (on the west side of Seven Mile Creek near its mouth), wudo'kan (in the marsh a mile from the last and east of Seven Mile Creek), iwunau'ts (on the western side of a little creek emptying into Klamath Lake two miles east of Recreation post office (1913-1924) and extending along the marsh shore to the northern side of Pelican Bay), duno'ksi (an open space overlooking the northern end of Pelican Bay), e'o'kai (a few hundred yards up Four Mile Creek on the left bank), wa'lo'kdi (above the last mentioned on the opposite side of the creek), wak'a'k (south of the high ridge south of Odessa post office 1902-1919), gai'loks or gaila'lks (on the point south of Odessa, or more probably between Howard and Shoalwater Bays), stokmatc (at Eagle Point), to which should perhaps be added: e'o'kak (on Wood River, toward the mountains), and c'ukwa'lksi (on the east side of Wood River, and possibly the same site as the other).

V. iu'la'lo$_n$kni (the people of Klamath Falls (Link River) and the eastern shore of Klamath Lake), including the following villages: kɛt!ai'ksi (extending southward from a promontory two miles or so northwest of Modoc Point), suwiaka'eks (at Modoc Point), iula'u (on the east side of Klamath Lake), diu'wiaks (at the railroad point Ouxy), kau'omot (a half mile south of the preceding on the lake shore), ditk!aks (at a hot spring known as Barclay Spring near the last mentioned), jolwa'l (at Rattlesnake Point at Algoma), wuk!l'twas (on Buck Island in Klamath Lake), lama'tcksi (on the point east of Buck Island), k!su'nk!si (three-fourths of a mile south of the preceding on the shore of Klamath Lake), iwau'wone (on both sides of Link River at the highway bridge), iu''lalo$_n$e (at the mouth of Klamath River), weka'els (on the shore of Klamath Lake a mile west of the mouth of Klamath River), wutñana'koks (at one end of a little marsh (now drained) on the west side of Klamath Lake), iup!a'tona (at the other end of the same marsh), woksa'lks (on the north shore of Wokas marsh near Klamath Lake), de'ktco$_n$ks (on the west shore of Klamath Lake opposite Buck Island), sa'stitka'-wals (at Squaw Point).

History: The Klamaths apparently go back over 10,000 years as evidenced by carbon dating of artifacts found in protected caves and under volcanic pumice.

The name, "The Klamath Tribe" today is a legal term which encompasses three tribes: Klamath, Modoc and Yahooshkin Snakes, also called Paiutes, as well as some Pit River whose ancestors had been enslaved by the Klamath and Modoc raids. Lowdon mentions a renegade band of Paiutes called Bannocks, related to, but not a part of Bannocks of Idaho (which see) who roamed this part of Oregon on horseback and were killers and raiders against other tribes, as well as against whites, for which the Klamaths and Modocs should not be blamed.

Klamath families tended to work together in whatever needed to be done without too much division between men's work and women's work. They were continually busy in this harsh, changeable climate, and developed a distinctive culture different from that of the east coast and plains Indians; also a different way of life from those of the north and west of the Cascades. The men were hunters, fishermen, traders, and warriors when needed. Women fished, gathered wocus, camas roots, eggs, berries, wild plums, seeds and other available foods in season, much of which they dried in the sun for winter storage. They also cut tules to make sleeping mats, sandals, baskets, clothing and cone-shaped summer houses called wukeplaks. They used dugout canoes which they propelled by long poles against the shallow lake bottom for gathering lake foods. Wocus *(Nymphaeaceae)* water lily. The pod a common Klamath food harvested in summer. (Seeds baked over fire until they pop open—looks like and tastes like popcorn.) The dugouts were sunk to the lake bottom for winter protection and raising them was one of the spring chores.

In the early 1850s the Army Corps of Topographical Engineers had been commissioned to search for suitable routes for railroads. An expedition of surveyors, guarded by over 100 troops, as well as packers who carried all the equipment including trade goods for the Indians, and also the staple foods, entered "Klamath country" south of the present-day city of Klamath Falls and proceeded north toward the Columbia River. This is popularly referred to as the Williamson and Abbot railroad expedition. Lt. Henry L. Abbot of the Topographical Engineers prepared an extensive report under the title *Explorations For A Railroad From the Sacramento River to the Columbia River.* (Although published in 1856 and long out of print, it appears in Appendix to the editor's book *Railroading in Southern Oregon.*) Abbot often related about Indians hiding in the trees and brush as well as Indians stealing mules. The year was 1855. Abbot describes the activities of August 21 when the surveyors surprised two Indians on the edge of Klamath Marsh. The Indians could not understand these strangers meant no harm so they "escaped as soon as possible." Shortly thereafter, the party reached a collection of Indian huts built near the edge of the water but the "two friends" had gotten to the village earlier, alerted the people and all had disappeared, even leaving their cooking fires burning with food at hand. All the troops had been ordered to leave the Indians' property strictly untouched. Accordingly, the Indians, who had been peering through the tules of the marsh from their dugout canoes, "began to doubt our hostile character and sent in a few squaws as an experiment." The surveyors gave the Indians gifts which seemed to wilt fears of trouble so large numbers of men entered the army camp with overtures of friendship. Abbot wrote, "We distrusted them. . . kept a close watch upon our animals during the night."

From the report:

August 22.—This morning many Indians came into camp. They were all well dressed in blankets and buckskin, and were armed with bows and arrows and a few fire-arms. Their intercourse with the Oregon settlements had taught many of them to speak the Chinook, or Jargon language, and one had a slight knowledge of English. They owned many horses, some of which were valuable animals. No offer would tempt them to sell any.

Near the spot where we were encamped, the marsh was not more than a mile in width; but it extended an indefinite distance towards the east, and the Indians informed us that the journey round it was very long, and without water. They volunteered to show us a natural causeway to the other side; but it proved too miry for pack mules. Our new friends all declared that the best trail to the Des Chutes valley led round the western side of the marsh. A large number of Indians accompanied us. These savages were intelligent.

August 23.—This morning we started with a large retinue of savages. The trail led through open pine timber for about a mile, and then entered a fine, grassy meadow which extended towards the north to Klamath marsh. About three miles from camp we reached Klamath river, here a sluggish stream divided into two branches by a narrow island. The water rose to the backs of the smaller mules, and Liet. Williamson employed the Indians to transport the packs across in canoes. This the squaws, who perform all the work, did by paddling round the northern end of the island. After paying their husbands with red blankets, beads, and vermilion, which they appear to highly prize, we continued our course through the grassy meadow until we reached a clear, ice-cold stream flowing through open timber. Here we encamped.

August 24.—This morning the Indians left us.

Congress established the Oregon Territory in 1848. Two years later the Indians met the first serious encroachment by whites when the U.S. Oregon Donation Land Act was passed. This Act failed to recognize agreements with the Indians. It provided that each adult U.S. citizen would be granted 320 acres of free land in the Oregon Territory. This brought an influx of white settlers who took over Indian land, killed and scared away game, thus the settlers became targets for retaliation by the Indians.

There were also warlike as well as peace factions among the whites. Colonel Drew in Jacksonville, southern Oregon's largest town, advocated harsh treatment and presided over some hangings. Ben Wright, from Yreka, led raids against Indians then planned a "peace party" at which he planned to trick the Indians into eating poisoned meat. Someone warned the Indians so the Indians didn't show up. On the other hand, a fur trader insisted the Indians would always have been peaceful except for the actions of some whites who just wanted to kill Indians for no reason. As antagonisms developed between the Indians and settlers, the whites pushed the government to move the Indians to a reservation. The Indians were further enraged in 1863 when Fort Klamath, a new military post, was set up on Klamath land between Wood River and what became known as Fort Creek.

In 1864 the Klamaths and the Modocs ceded their land to the government in exchange for life on a reservation—but without the bad parts being explained to them.

Under white man's rule on the reservation, all Indians were registered and given American names. The Indians were not to use their own names any longer. The activities and life on the reservation was intended to change the manner of living in all areas of Indian life. This was a culture shock of major proportions that the government, in its infinite wisdom, failed to recognize. The tribe was directed to give up hunting and fishing and the women could no longer gather the fruits of the earth. All were assertively directed to learn "white man's language" and adopt the religion of the white conquerors. Henceforth Indians were to dress in "civilized" clothing as worn by the whites. Employees of the reservation were not, for the most part, very carefully chosen and few knew anything about the Indians. The few employees who did understand did everything possible to help the tribe with the transition. But others held the Indians only in contempt and regarded them only as "savages."

An aboriginal culture gave way to conjugal family life. Chiefs became more important. The Agency, after a lot of pressure from leaders, permitted the formation of a tribal council which incorporated chiefs and sub-chiefs and encouraged the election of leaders. In time, the reservation became divided. It separated into the upper end folks moving east, and the lower end to the west along the lakes. In 1870 a sub-agency, Yainax, became established on the Sprague River about 40 miles east of Klamath Falls. (This is seen on current road maps as the villages of Sprague River and, a little further east, Beatty.) Schonchin and Monchn-kasgiek shared chiefships. Schonchin, for the Modocs, most of whom had moved east from Modoc Point, on Upper Klamath Lake, and Monshnkasgiek for the Klamaths and Paiutes already there.

The Modocs became displeased in their interaction with the Klamaths. In years earlier the two tribes had formed joint raiding parties and ventured to the Pit River band, north of Redding, California, to capture slaves. These trips had been annual events. The slaves provided wives and some slaves were traded at The Dalles or in Oregon City. (Slaves eventually acquired equal status in the Klamath Tribe.) But in the 1860s the Modocs claimed discrimination by the Klamaths and decided to move away.

There had previously been a treaty drawn between the Modocs and California Director of Indian Affairs, Elijah Steele, giving them the northern California area around Lost River and the Lava Beds and all the Tule Lake area. Apparently Steele had no authority to do this, thus the treaty was never ratified. Nobody told the Modocs.

Under the leadership of "chief" Kintpuash, who had been named "Captain Jack" by some burleys in Yreka, the Modocs went to their old area in California. Although this move had the good wishes and official agreement from General E.S.B. Canby and the Oregon Indian Superintendent, each thinking the move was for the better interests of both tribes, the request was denied due to complaints of the whites. This became a standoff. The Modocs would not return to the reservation, which resulted in the Modoc Indian War. This warfare, and the outcome to Captain Jack and others, is told in the pages for the Modoc Tribe. The Klamaths took no part in the Modoc Indian War.

An historical summary of some events affecting the Klamath Indians:

By 1888 the reservation had grown in size to 1,056,000 acres. A resurvey in 1900 included additional land apparently missed earlier but the acreage discovered was not given to the Indians but was paid for by the government.

Because of legal challenges following the Oregon Central Military Road Company's contract with the State of Oregon to build a road across the reservation, the Dawes Allotment Act of 1887 was nearly one hundred years late in taking effect for the Klamaths. As Lynn Schonchin, a teacher and historian wrote, "Total allotments numbered 1,624 to individual Indians on the Klamath Reservation. The Dawes Act sought to make land owners and farmers out of Indians."

In 1953 Congress passed a resolution to terminate federal regulations and services with all tribes in the United States. The next year, Public Law 587 terminated federal services to the Klamaths and liquidated tribal assets including the land. The tribe rejected the Termination Act, but Congress sold the land and divided the proceeds to members of the tribe that chose to withdraw. Congress purchased 86 percent of the land and created the Winema (Wynee-ma) National Forest. About 30 percent of the tribe wanted to stay and thus kep 135,000 acres which was placed under trust in the United States National Bank of Oregon. When remaining members voted to end the trust in 1969, this land was sold and became a part of Winema National Forest.

In a highly contested case, the U.S. Supreme Court held that the Klamath Tribe's traditional hunting, fishing and gathering rights had been guaranteed by the original treaty, thus in 1974 this became a treaty right that survived termination.

The tribe established the Klamath Indian Game Commission to oversee the rights and hired a wildlife biologist and enforcement officers. In 1979 the tribe won a water-rights dispute (*U.S.* vs. *Adair*) which ensures there will be a minimum flow of water for protection and enhancement of fish and wildlife.

The tribe assertively went to work to gain restoration of federal recognition and on August 18, 1986, Public Law 99-398 was enacted that restored the tribe. But this was all on paper. No land was granted for a tribal home. Nevertheless, immediate emphasis was given to economic development towards self-sufficiency. A health service program was developed for medical, dental and housing rehabilitation. Special educational needs were implemented at all levels including adult vocational training. A social services program went into effect to coordinate child welfare, outreach, substance abuse and mental health services. In addition, there are continuing efforts in wildlife management, stream rehabilitation and habitat studies in conjunction with U.S. Forest Service timber sales. The tribe established a fish hatchery.

The Klamath Tribe has been affected by almost every national policy dealing with Indians and through it all the tribe has survived.

It will be of interest to observe the impact of organized religion on the Klamath Indians.

The various religious persuasions, on observing the implementation of the reservation system, recognized that the reservations held a captive audience. Accordingly, missionaries literally grabbed the first trains to the closest point to the reservations to claim the "heathen." The competition became so merciless that the Indian Office in Washington, D.C., called a halt then divided the reservations among the denominations, allowing only one to be on a given reservation. The Indian Office assigned the Klamath Reservation to the Methodists. The local Shaman gave way to Indian ministers who had been trained by the white missionaries. Any healing, once claimed the domain of the medicine men, was turned over to the Agency Health Service.

It took a long time for Indians to give up their traditional religious dances and sweat lodges, especially the "ghost dance." This was supposed to attain the demise of the whites. Those Indians killed would return to life and the land would revert to the status it had been before the arrival of whites who ruined it.

As for the Klamaths, many accepted the teachings of the Methodists, but some went to off-reservation churches. These were primarily Roman Catholic and the fundamentalistic. But during all these years, the Methodists have prevailed. In the 1920s, in a deed signed by President Warren G. Harding, the church was given title to 110 acres of reservation land. This acreage, near Beatty, was held in trust by the Methodist Board of Global Ministries. The church building at Beatty, about 50 miles east of Klamath Falls, is on one corner of the acreage. In 1987, the Board of Global Ministries noted the restoration of the tribe, but observed the new law failed to provide any land. The Board decided to return the trust land to the Indians. On December 4, 1988, the Chairman of the Board of Global Ministries came to Beatty. In a special ceremony attended by about 150 Indians, he handed the deed to tribal officers.

The Methodists consider their presence as a permanent mission with the Klamaths. They maintain regular worship services as well as supportive activities in Chiloquin, Fort Klamath, at the settlement of Williamson River and at Beatty, even though most of the folks at Beatty have moved away. The membership there dwindled to 13 and, for a period, the minister drove 80 miles each Sunday to hold a service for a single worshipper. Indeed, this appears as evidence of "possibility thinking" by the Methodists. As for "supportive activities," the Beatty church held a turkey shoot for the first time in years. This was followed, in early 1989, with a dinner for all the tribe's elders. Does the husband/wife team of ministers who ride circuit between the churches believe in a positive religious future for the

Klamath Tribe? It's happening, they assert.
Population:

1780	800 (Mooney, 1928)
1826	1,200 (Peter Skene Ogden)
1868	374 (Hodge)
1880	1,125 (Klamath and Modoc)
1887	673
1905	755 (Includes former slaves and others)
1910	696 (U.S. Census)
1911	791
1923	1,201 (Reservation, includes Klamath and Modoc)
1930	2,034 (Klamath and Modoc—U.S. Census)
1937	1,912 (Klamath—U.S. Office of Indian Affairs)
1987	(See Appendix)

Names by which remembered: Name of county; city (ZIP 97601, 97603); river; marsh; mountains; strait; Fort Klamath (city, ZIP 97626).

Kutish
Also called:

Ci-sta'-qwût-mê' tunne', Mishikwutmetunne name, meaning "people dwelling on the stream called Shista."
Lower Umpqua, or Umpwua, popular name.
Tu'kwil-ma'-k'i, Alsea name.

Linguistic group: Yakonan
Location: On Lower Umpqua River.
Villages:

Chitlatamus	Paiuiyunitthai
Chukhuiyathl	Skakhaus
Chukukh	Takhaiya
Chupichnushkuch	Thukhita
Kaiyuwuntsunitthai	Tkimeye
Khuwaihus	Tsalila
Kthae	Tsetthim
Kuiltsh	Tsiakhaus
Mikulitsh	Tsunakthiamittha
Misum	Wuituthlaa
Ntsiyamis	

84

Kutish usually classed with Siuslaw (which see).
Population:

> All Yakonan stock:
> 1780   6,000 (Mooney, 1928)
> 1930   9 (U.S. Census)
> The Kutish are not enumerated separately.

Latgawa
Meaning: "Those living in the uplands."
Also called:

> Walumskni, by the Klamath.

Linguistic group: Takilman, probably part of Shastan
Location: Upper Rogue River near Table Rocks (also village of Table Rock—post office 1872-1906) vicinity confluence of the river with Stuart (Stewart) Creek (now Bear Creek), the area near Central Point; a city about eight miles southwest near present city of Jacksonville.
Population: (See Takilma)

Lohim
(See Paiute, Northern)
Location: On Willow Creek which is mentioned by Lewis and Clark as a "riverlet" that flows into the Columbia in Gilliam County, on today's maps at Heppner Junction with Interstate Freeway 84. The Lohim never made a treaty with the government, thus are generally referred to as "renegades." They were assigned to the Umatilla Reservation.
Population:

> 1870   114

Luckiamute (Lakmiut)
"Alakema'yuk, Atfalati name; "Suck-a-mier, Chelukimaukes.
Linguistic group: Kalapooian, Calapooya dialect
Location: On Luckiamute River.

Subdivisions:

> Ampalamuyu, on Luckiamute River.
> Mohawk, on Mohawk River.
> Tsalakmiut, on Luckiamute River.
> Tsamiak, near Luckiamute River.
> Tsantatawa, south of Luckiamute River.
> Tsantuisha, on Luckiamute River.

Population:

> 1905   28 (Hodge)
> 1910   8 (U.S. Census)

Names by which remembered: Luckiamute River.

Miluk (Miluk Coos)
(See Hanis)
Location: Mouth of Coquille River (city of Bandon).
Villages:

> Miluk (Mulluk) north side of Coquille River at site of former village of Randolph (post office 1859-1893) about three miles from the ocean
> Nasumi, south side of Coquille River near present city of Bandon (ZIP 97411).

Population: (See Hanis).

Mishikhwutmetunne
("people who live on the stream called Mishi"— Coquille River).
Also called:

> Coquille, or Upper Coquille, from their habitat.
> De-d'á tené, Tutuni name, meaning "people by the northern water."
> Ithalé teni, Umpqua name.
> Kukwil', Alsea name (from Coquille).

Linguistic group: Athapascan
Location: Upper Coquille River.

Villages:

Chockreletan, near the forks of
   Coquille River
Chuntshataatunne
Duldulthawaiame
Enitunne
Ilsethlthawaiame
Katomemetunne
Khinukhtunne
Khwesthtunne, next above city of Coquille
Kimestunne
Kthukhwestunne
Kthunataachuntunne
Meshtshe
Nakhituntunne
Nakhochatunne
Natarghiliitunne
Natsushltatunne
Nilestunne
Rghoyinestunne
Sathlrekhtun
Sekhushtuntunne
Sunsunnestunne
Sushltakhotthatunne
Thlkwantiyatunne
Thltsharghiliitunne
Thltsusmetunne
Thlulchikhwutmetunne
Timethltunne
Tkhlunkhastunne, next to the Kusan people
   and below city of Coquille
Tsatarghekhetunne
Tthinatlitunne, at the site of Coquille
Tulwutmetunne
Tuskhlustunne
Tustatunkhuushi. Drucker (1937) recorded besides:
Hwesthtun (perhaps partly Kusan)
Natgrilitun
Stonerutltutl, a suburb of Natgrilitun
Tlunhoshtun, said to have come from Umpqua.

Population:

1861   225 (B.I.A.)

87

1884   (no count, but on Siletz Reservation)
1910   15 (recorded under name Upper Coquille—
    U.S. Census)

Modoc

Mowatodkni ("People of the south").
Also called:

> Aigspaluma, Nez Percé name for all Indians on Klamath
>   Reservation and in the vicinity.
> La-la-cas, said to be the original name.
> Lutmáwi, by a part of the Pit River Indians.
> Lutuami, Ilmawi name.
> P$_x$ánai, Yreka Shasta name.
> Saidoka, Shoshoni name.

Linguistic group: Lutuamian
Location: Both sides of Oregon-California state line. On
Little Klamath Lake, Modoc Lake, Tule Lake, Lost River
Valley, Clear Lake. Some ventured to Goose Lake.
Subdivisions: Most important bands are believed to
have been at Little Klamath Lake, Tule Lake and Lost River
Valley.
Villages: (*Note: Rhett Lake was the original name for
Tule Lake, but with the relocation of Lost River the lake
has all but dried up. In fact, the lake is completely gone in
Oregon. A village, Tule Lake, Oregon, had a post office on
and off from 1893 to 1922. The place, Tule Lake, just over
the border in California (ZIP 96134) more commonly comes
to mind than the former town in Oregon. —Editor*)

> Agawesh, on lower Klamath Lake, Calif., and on Hot Creek.
> Chakawech, near Yaneks, on Sprague River, Klamath
>   Reservation.
> Kalelk, on the north shore of Tule (Rhett) Lake.
> Kawa, at Yaneks on Sprague River.
> Keshlakchuis, on the southeast side of Tule (Rhett) Lake, Calif.
> Keuchishkeni, on Hot Creek near Little Klamath Lake, Calif.
> Kumbatuash (with Klamath), southwest of Tule (Rhett)
>   Lake, Calif., extending from the lake shore to the
>   lava beds.
> Leush, on the north side of Tule (Rhett) Lake, Oreg.
> Nakoshkeni, at the junction of Lost River with Tule Lake.

Nushaltkagakni, at the headwaters of Lost River near Bonanza
Pashka, on the northwest shore of Tule (Rhett) Lake.
Shapashkeni, on the southeast side of Little Klamath
  Lake, Calif.
Sputuishkeni, on Lower Klamath Lake, Calif.
Stuikishkeni, on the north side of Little Klamath Lake.
Waisha, on Lost River, 3 or 4 miles northwest of Tule Lake,
  and near the hills that culminate in Laki Peak.
Wachamshwash, on Lost River near Tule (Rhett) Lake,
  in Klamath County.
Welwashkeni, on the southeast side of Tule Lake, at
  Miller's Farm, Calif.
Wukakeni, on the east side of Tule Lake, Calif.
Yaneks (with Klamath and Shoshoni), along middle
  Sprague River, Lake County.
Yulalona (with Klamath), at the site of the present Linkville.

History: The Modoc came into contact with whites in comparatively late times, and acquired an unfortunate reputation from frequent conflicts with immigrants in which atrocities were committed on both sides. In 1864 the Modoc and Klamath (see Klamath) together ceded their territory to the United States and retired to Klamath Reservation, but the Modoc were never contented there and made persistent efforts to return to their old country. Finally, in 1870, a chief named Kintpuash, known to whites as Captain Jack, led the more turbulent element of the Modocs back to the California border and refused to return. The first attempt to bring the runaways back precipitated the Modoc War of 1872-73. The Modoc retreated to the lava beds of northern California and for several months refused all demands they return to the reservation. The Indians found the natural fortification of the lava area to their advantage and were able to frustrate attacks that were intended to overcome them. In April of 1873, peace commissioners were trying to negotiate with the Modocs when two of these men were assassinated. One was Brig. Gen. Edward R. S. Canby, Commanding General of the Department of the Columbia. The other was Rev. Dr. Eleazer Thomas, member of the peace commission. Both were murdered when under a truce flag at the lava beds. In that instant, the Modocs lost two of

EXECUTION OF CAPTAIN JACK

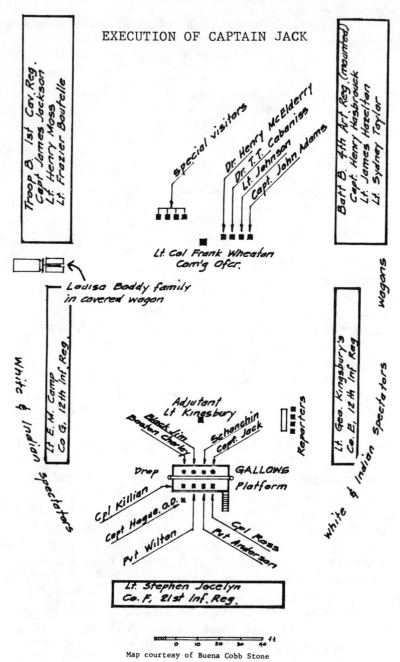

Map courtesy of Buena Cobb Stone

their staunchest champions. Although the military commander, General Canby, was friendly to the Indians and wanted
no war, on demands of the Indian Agent at the reservation,
the cavalry was sent to return the Modoc to the reservation
in peace if possible, or with force if needed.

Of the six Modocs tried and found guilty of the
murders of the commissioners, all were sentenced to hang at
Fort Klamath. Hodge (1905) errs in the statement that
"Kintpuash [Captain Jack] and five other leaders were
hanged...October [3rd], 1873." A Presidential pardon
changed the death penalties of two of the six to life
imprisonment within hours of the scheduled executions, thus
while a giant gallows intended for six had been constructed,
six coffins stored under the platform and six graves dug,
only four were used. Most accounts of this event end here
with the possible exception of Landrum. In his book
Guardhouse, Gallows and Graves, he suggests, with good
evidence, that Army Surgeon Dr. Henry J. McElderry
removed the heads of the hanged and sent them to the Army
Medical Museum in Washington, D.C., where these skulls
joined the collection of about 3,000 others. Are the heads
there today? In 1949 the Smithsonian Institution Department of Anthropology, which inherited the Army collection, wrote it was "probable" the skulls of these Modocs
were in the museum. These heads would be those of Captain
Jack, Boston Charley, Schonchin John and Black Jim. But
as the skulls were not identified when received, no identity
now, nearly 120 years later, seems possible.

On the completion of the army's involvement with the
Modocs, the remnants of the tribe were distributed between
the Quapaw Reservation in Indian Territory (Oklahoma)
and the Klamath Reservation.

It has been claimed that the Modoc Indian War was the
most costly Indian conflict with a price tag of more than
$500,000, and 1,200 troops, to subdue about 60 Indians.
There were 83 whites killed.

Population:

1780   400 (Mooney, 1928)

```
1864  700
1890   84 (Quapaw Reservation, Oklahoma)
      151 (Klamath Reservation)
1905   56 (Oklahoma)
      223 (Klamath Reservation)
1910   33 (Oklahoma—U.S. Census)
      212 (Oregon—U.S. Census)
       20 (California—U.S. Census)
        5 (Other states—U.S. Census)
1985  133 (Oklahoma—Yenne)
1987  (See Appendix)
```

Names by which remembered: The name is perpetuated by the Modoc Indian War which occurred in the Lava Beds National Monument in Siskiyou County, California; national forest; county in California; Modoc Point on Klamath Lake. Also towns in Arkansas, Georgia, Louisiana, Ohio, South Carolina, Illinois, Indiana, Kansas.

Molala (Molalla)

Whether the name of the tribe came from the name, Molalla River, or the other way around is unknown.

Also called:

> Amolélish, by the Kalapuya.
> Kúikni, by the Klamath.
> Láti-u or La'tiwe, their own name.
> Ya'-ide'sta, by the Umpqua.

Linguistic group: Shapwailutan, Waillatpuan division
Location: In the valleys of the Molalla and Santiam Rivers, Willamette Valley south of Oregon City.
Subdivisions:

> Chakankni, in a region northwest of Klamath Lake, west of Crater Lake and in the extreme upper Rogue River headwaters.
> Chimbuiha, on headwaters of Santiam River.
> Mukanti, on western slopes of Cascade Mountains, presumably on the Molalla River.

History: When first encountered the Molalla lived in the Cascade Mountains between Mounts Hood and Scott and on western slopes in both Washington and Oregon. According to Cayuse tradition, the Molalla lived with them south of the Columbia River but due to wars with hostile tribes became separated. The dialect of the Molalla, while related to that of the Cayuse, is distinct, so much so that the separation was in all probability in remote times. Hodge claims the Molalla discovered the lush vegetation along the Molalla River and drove out the occupants, assuming title to the place.

Population:

```
1849  100
1877  a few, Grande Ronde Reservation
1881  20 in mountains west of Klamath Lake
1910  31 (U.S. Census)
```

Names by which remembered: Molalla, a city (ZIP 97038), river.

Multnomah

"Ne'maLnomax," (down river)

Also called:

> Mulknomans by Lewis and Clark.
>
> Wappato, originally the Cree or Chippewa name of a bulbous root (*Sagitiaria variabilis*) used as food by the Indians of the west and northwest. It means literally "white fungus." It passed into the Chinook jargon with the meaning "potato" and became applied to Sauvies Island in Columbia River, at the mouth of the Willamette, and the Indian tribes living on or near it. It was so used by Lewis and Clark, though there was little or no political connection between the numerous bands so designated.

Linguistic group: Chinookian

Location: East side of Sauvie Island in the Columbia River.

Subdivisions:

> Cathlacomatup, on the south side of Sauvie Island on a slough of Willamette River.

Cathlacumup on the west bank of the lower mouth
of the Willamette River and claiming as their
territory the bank of the Columbia from there
to Deer Island.

Cathlanaquiah, on the southwest side of Sauvie Island.

Clahnaquah, on Sauvie Island.

Claninnata, on the southwest side of Sauvie Island.

Kathlaminimin, at the south end of Sauvie Island,
later said to have become associated with the
Cathlacumup and Nemoit.

Multnomah, on the upper end of Sauvie Island.

Nechacokee, on the south bank of Columbia River
a few miles below Quicksand (Sandy) River.

Nemalquinner, at the falls of the Willamette but with
a temporary house on the north end of Sauvie
Island.

Shoto, on the north side of Columbia River, a short
distance from it and nearly opposite the mouth
of the Willamette.

History: The tribe was discovered by Lewis and Clark
on their westward journey in 1805 when they noted in their
Journal on November 4 a village of Indians which they
named "Mulknomans." This name they originated from the
name "Mulknomah," for the river they observed entering
the Columbia from the south—the Willamette River. The
explorers, on ascending the Columbia the next year, used
the letter "t" in the name and recorded it that way on their
maps. The name for the Indians thus became "Multnomah."

Population:

1780   3,600 (Mooney, 1928)
1806   800
1910   The tribe seems to have been absorbed with
       others of the area and reported as "Chinook."
       (U.S. Census)

Names by which remembered: County, town (post
office 1912-1940); river channel; falls (620 ft. drop) on
Columbia River; mountain claimed to have been giant
volcano in Cascades in pre-historic era. Wappato, secondar-
ily applied to these Indians: an intermittent lake (see

Atfalati); also a name for Sauvie Island (post office Sauvie's Island 1866-1881) with spelling "Sapato" (not recognized by McArthur) plausibly referring to Wapato Lake and to city in Washington (ZIP 98951).

Naltunnetunne
Small Athapascan tribe on Oregon coast between Tutitni and Chetco apparently included with Tututni (which see).

Neketemeuk (See Washington)

Nez Perce
Location: In eastern Oregon Wallowa County. (See Idaho)

Paiute, Northern
Location: Southeastern Oregon extending as far north as Powder River and upper John Day River. (See Nevada)

Rogue River Indians
A name given to all tribes along the Rogue River in Southern Oregon, particularly when referring to the "Rogue River Indian Wars" of the 1850s.
Names by which remembered: River in Curry, Jackson, Josephine, Klamath counties; river in Polk County so named because Indians from tribes along the southern Oregon river were moved to the Grande Ronde Reservation and took up housekeeping along the river; city (ZIP 97537); a community college.

Santiam
Also called:

Aha'lpam, by the Atfalati Kalapuya.

Linguistic group: Kalapooian, Calapooya dialect
Location: Along the Santiam River to confluence with the Willamette River and up the Yamhill River.

Villages:

> Chamifu, on Yamhill River. Chanchampenau, east of Willa-
> mette River.
> Chanchantu, location not specified.
> Chantkaip, below the junction of the Santiam forks.

History: The only history that seems available is from
Hodge who wrote that the Santiam Indians were transport-
ed to the Grande Ronde Reservation on an unknown date.
Zucker only implies their location in the Willamette Valley.
Population:

> 1906   23 (reservation)
> 1910   9

Names by which remembered: A river, a town (post
office 1887-1906).

Shasta
This California tribe ventured into the Jenny Creek
area in Jackson County, Oregon. (See California)

Silela
Lewis and Clark identified the Silelas as a branch of the
Kuitsh (which see) on lower Umpqua River and entered the
population as 1,200.

Siletz
Also called:

> Celeste, Neselitch, Sailetc.
> K'cu-qwic'tûnne, Naltunne name.
> K'qlo-qwec tûnne, Chastacosta name.
> Tsa Shádsh amín, name used by Luckiamute Kalapuyas.

Linguistic group: Salishan
Location: Along the Siletz River to the bay.
Population:

> Not recorded separately.
> 1930   72 Salishan Indians including Siletz (U.S. Census).

Names by which remembered: Southernmost tribe of the Salishan linguistic group; a river; a town (ZIP 97380).

Siltcoos

Location: Around Siltcoos Lake. Plausibly a village of the Kuitsch, "Tsiakhaus." The lake earlier spelled Tsiltcoos.

Names by which remembered: The lake, a village (post office 1916-1963).

Siuslaw

Also called:

Shiastuckle
Saoustla
Saliutla
Saiustla.

Linguistic group: Yakonan
Location: Along Siuslaw River.
Villages:

Chimuksaich	Matsnikth
Hauwiyat	Mithlausmintthai
Hilakwitiyus	Paauwis
Khachtais	Pia
Khaikuchum	Pilumas
Khaiyumitu	Pithlkwutsiaus
Khakhaich	Skhutch
Khalakw	Stthukhwich
Kumiyus	Thlachaus
Kumkwu	Thlekuauas
Kupimithlta	Tikewachi
Kuskussu	Tsahais
Kwsichichu (south of Eugene)	Tsatauwis
Kwulhauunnich	Tsiekhaweyathl
Kwultsaiya	Waitus
Kwunnumis	Wetsiaus
Kwuskwemus	Yukhwustitu

Population:

1910   7 (U.S. Census)

97

Names by which remembered: A river, a town (post office 1852-1898).

Skillot
Location: Both sides of the Columbia River opposite the mouth of the Cowlitz river. (See Washington)

Snake (Listed under Northern Paiute in Nevada).

Takelma
("Those living along the river").
Also called:

> Illinois River Indians.
> Kyu'-kutc hitclûm, Alsea name meaning "people
>   far down the stream (or country)."
> Lowland Takelma, of Berreman (1937).
> Na-tcté tûnne, Naltunne name.
> Rogue River Indians, from their habitat.

Linguistic group: Takilman, with the Latgawa
Swanton suggests the Takilmas were distantly related to Shastas of northern California. This was earlier established by Hodge.
Location: along the Rogue River from above confluence with the Illinois river to about Grants Pass as well as along tributaries of the Rogue to upper Cow Creek. The Takilmas were known along the Illinois River south of Grants pass, and near moth of Applegate River.
Villages:

> Hashkushtun, on the south side of Rogue River.
> Hudedut, at the forks of Rogue River and Applegate River.
> Kashtata, on the south side of Rogue River above Leaf Creek
>   and Galice Creek.
> Kthotaime, on the south side of Rogue River.
> Nakila, on the south side of Rogue River about 10 miles above
>   Yaasitun.
> Salwahka, near the mouth of Illinois River or one of its
>   tributaries.
> Seethltun, on the south side of Rogue River, the village nearest
>   the Chastacosta.

Sestikustun, on the south side of Rogue River.
Sewaathlchutun, ibid.
Shkashtun, ibid.
Skanowethltunne, ibid.
Talmamiche, ibid.
Talotunne, ibid.
Tthowache, on the south side of Rogue River near "Deep Rock."
Yaasitun, on the south side of Rogue River.
Yushlali, ibid.

The following names, probably covering in part the same towns, were recorded by Dr. Edward Sapir in 1906, and are enumerated from the Latgawa country downstream:

Hatil, east of Table Rock.
Gelyalk, below Table Rock.
Dilomi, near Rainie Falls on Rogue River.
Gwenpunk.
Hayaalbalsda.
Daktgamik.
Didalam, on the present site of Grants Pass, the county seat of Josephine County.
Daktsasin or Daldanik, on Rogue River near Jump Off Joe Creek.
Hagwal, on Cow Creek.
Somouluk.
Hatonk.

History: Culturally, the Takilma were allied with the Shasta who dwelled in northern California. The contact between tribes was such that they frequently intermarried.

The Takilma lived in an area rich in foods. These included fresh fish, camas root, a variety of wild berries and availability of wild game—large and small. The weather was not overly severe in winter, but summers could be in the high 90°-100°+F. range. Apparently the only cultivated crop was tobacco.

These Indians adorned their faces with "paint" probably made of vegetable dye in colors of red, black, and when on the war-path, white. Both men and women tattooed themselves. The social life seemed simple. Villages were small and all seemed to get along well together. Apparently a man became Chief because he had more wealth than the next man. Marriages were arranged by purchase of the bride with gifts to the father, who in turn sent gifts along with the young woman to the new husband. When a child was born, extra gratuity was sent to the woman's father. These marriages were nearly always from neighboring villages as there was a rule against any unions of near relatives. Polygamy was practiced but was expensive due to the second set of gifts needed to procure an additional wife. When death occurred, the body was buried in the ground. The graves were decorated with items valued by the deceased.

The Takilmas used considerable numbers of charms and medicinal recipes for incantations by their "medicine man." There was great belief in mythology. The most characteristic legends were the deeds of a hero, Dalkal, and the antics of Coyote.

Takilma Indians were involved in the Rogue Indian Wars and lost so many warriors that the tribe's numbers were severely reduced. Eventually, the tribe, along with other tribes, was exiled on the Grande Ronde and Siletz Reservations.

Speaking before Congress on May 30, 1860, General Joseph Lane stated:

> The Indians of Oregon and Washington...are able in war. They are as brave as any people on the face of the earth. I have never met men of more courage than the warriors of [Southern Oregon]....
> They are men of character, of much knowledge and great treachery. They are bold in war. They have never been whipped thoroughly in any fight they have had with the whites.

Population:

1780   500 (Mooney, 1928)
1910   1 (U.S. Census)

Names by which remembered: Town of Takilma (post office 1902-1958). With the Latgawa, the Takilma are noted for their unique language, being surrounded by Athapascans.

Talushtuntude
Linguistic group: Athapascan
Also called:

> Galice Creek Indians, from their habitat.
> Kû-lis'-kitc hitc'lûm, Alsea name.

History: This tribe was culturally associated with the Takilma (which see), but there was a language gap.
Location: Along Galice Creek and near confluence with Rogue River.
Population:

> 1856   18 (Siletz Reservation)
> 1937   42 (under name "Galice Creek" Indians—B.I.A.)

Tenino
Also called:

> Meli'-lema (own name)
> Warm Springs Indians, common official designation.

Linguistic group: Shapwailutan, Shahaptian branch
Subdivisions and villages:

> Kowasayee, on the north bank of Columbia River nearly opposite the mouth of the Umatilla.
> Ochechote or Uchichol, on the north bank of Columbia River, the exact region being uncertain though they derive their name from a rock near the mouth of the Deschutes River.
> Skinpah, on the north bank of Columbia River above the mouth of the Deschutes.
> Tapanash, on the north bank of Columbia River, near the mouth of the Deschutes and a little above Celilo, the name being later extended over most of the above bands.
> Tilkuni, between White and Warm Springs Reservations.
> Tukspush, on John Day River, and hence called often John Day Indians.
> Wahopum, on the north bank of Columbia River near the mouth of Olive Creek.
> Waiam, near the mouth of the Deschutes River.

History: Lewis and Clark mention Teninos in 1805. In 1855 they participated in the Wasco Treaty and moved to the Warm Springs Reservation. The tribe has been referred to as "Warm Springs Indians," but this includes various tribes that were settled there. Today, the Confederated Tribes of Warm Springs guides the life and activities of the reservation in conjunction with federal laws. This confederation has developed a major business and tourist center, which includes a lumber mill and a plywood plant, and one of Oregon's most popular resorts and convention centers—Kah-Nee-Ta.

When the Federal Writers Project book, *Oregon, End of the Trail*, was published in 1940, the remarks about the Warm Springs Reservation included: "covers 300,000 barren acres [where]...Tenino, Wasco, Paiute and Klickitat tribes were herded. [In 1940] 725 Indians live here on government rations since crops are too poor to support even this number of people." But when Secretary of the Interior A. H. H. Stuart reported in 1855, "...to tame a savage one must tie him down to the soil," Mr. Stuart had not reckoned with the eventual spirit of the Warm Springs Indians and their thirst for independence and what they could do about their situation. But it took many years. The reservation had been isolated until Highway 26 was routed through the center of it. With a road, the potential could be realized. With the inundation of the Celilo Falls fishing location on the Columbia, caused by the building of The Dalles Dam by the U.S. Army Corps of Engineers in 1957, the Indians received four million dollars in compensation. Although large doles of money to tribes in the past had usually been divided among the members, in this instance only a token amount was given each Indian. The rest was invested.

Under the guidance of the Tribal Council, money was invested in a comprehensive survey of human and natural resources at Oregon State College (now University) in 1960. During this period, Portland General Electric Company wanted to build power generating dams on two rivers, through the centers of which are the reservation boundaries. Agreements were reached, two dams were built, and the Confederated Tribes receives millions of dollars each year at this writing. In addition, a section of the contract on one of the dams allowed the Indians to install their own generator downstream, which they did, thus the reservation now has its own operating power project. And there are other enterprises too many to mention here, including two radio stations on the reservation. Everything is operated for the good of the Indians.

Population:

    1905   30 (Tenino only)
    1940   725 (Confederated Tribe, Warmsprings
           Reservation)
    1987   (See Appendix)

Names by which remembered: Tenino: city in Washington (ZIP 98589). Warm Springs: city (ZIP 97761); river; Indian Reservation.

Tillamook
"The people of Nehalem." (Nekelim)
Also called:

    Calamox
    Gillamooks
    Killamook
    Killamuck
    Higgahaldahu, Nestucca name
    Kyaukw, Alsea name
    Nsietshawas, so called by Hale (1846)
    Si ni'-te-li, Mishikwutmetunne name for this tribe and the
        Alsea, meaning "flatheads."

Linguistic group: Salishan
Location: Along the Oregon coast from Nehalem to Salmon Rivers.
Subdivisions and villages:

    Nehalem, on Nehalem River.
    Nestucca, on Nestucca Bay and the streams flowing into it.

103

Salmon River, on the river of that name.
Tillamook, on Tillamook Bay and the streams flowing into it,
including the following villages enumerated by Lewis and
Clark: Chishucks (at the mouth of Tillamook River),
Chucktin (the southernmost Tillamook village, on a creek
emptying into Tillamook Bay), Kilherhursh (at the entrance
of Tillamook Bay), Kilherner (on Tillamook Bay, at the
mouth of a creek two miles from Kilherhursh), Towerquot-
ten (on a creek emptying into Tillamook Bay).

History: The culture of the Tillamooks differed from
the north coast Salish and was influenced by tribes of
northern California coastal areas. Lewis and Clark reported
the Tillamooks occupied eight villages. These Indians
enjoyed a year-round harvest of fish of many kinds from
the rivers emptying into the bay and from the ocean, as well
as oysters and clams in abundance.

Population:

1805	2,200 (Lewis and Clark)
1845	400 (Wilkes)
1949	200 (Lane)
1987	(See Appendix)

Names by which remembered: The bay; a county; city
(ZIP 97141); a cape on the sea-front, Tillamook Head; an
offshore rock with lighthouse (1881-1959).

Tututni
Also called:

H'lilush, Nestucca name.
Lower Rogue River Indians, or Rogue River Indians, from their
habitat. Tálemaya, Umpqua name.
Ta-qu'-qûc-ce, Chetco name, meaning "northern language."

Linguistic group: Athapascan
Location: Lower Rogue River and both sides of its
mouth at the ocean.
Villages:

On the north coast of Rogue River:

Chemetunne, popularly called Joshuas, just north of Rogue River.

Kaltsergheatunne, at Port Orford.

Kosotshe, between Port Orford and Sixes Creek, perhaps earlier on Flores Creek.

Kwatami, on or near Sixes River.

Kthukwutttune.

Kthutetmeseetuttun, just north of Rogue River.

Kwusathlkhuntunne, said to have been at the mouth of Mussel Creek, 5 miles south of Humbug Mountain.

Natutshltunne, between Coquille River and Flores Creek.

Niletunne, the first village south of the Miluk village of Nasumi, south of Coquille River.

Yukichetunne, on Euchre Creek.

On Rogue River:

Chetlesiyetunne, on the north side.

Enitunne, near the mouth of a souther affluent of Rogue River.

Etaatthetunne.

Kunechuta.

Kushetunne, on the north side.

Mikonotunne, on the north side 14 miles from its mouth.

Nakatkhaitunne, on the north side of Rogue River.

Targheliichetunne, on the north side.

Targhutthotunne, near the coast.

Testthitun, on the north side.

Thechuntunne, on the north side.

Thethlkhttunne, or Chastacosta, on the north side.

On or near the coast south of Rogue River:

Chetleschantunne, on Pistol River and the headlands from the coast 6 miles south of Rogue River.

Khainanaitetunne.

Kheerghia, about 25 miles south of Pistol River.

Khwaishtunnetunne, near the mouth of a small stream locally called Wishtenatin, after the name of the settlement, that enters the Pacific about 10 miles south of Pistol River, at a place later known as Hustenate.

Natthutunne, on the south side of Rogue River.

Nuchumatuntunne, on the north side of Rogue River near the mouth.

Sentethltun, on the south side of Rogue River and perhaps at its mouth.

Skumeme, on the south side of Rogue River near its mouth.

Tsetintunne, the highest of 4 villages on a stream emptying into
Rogue River near its mouth.

Tsetuttunne.

Drucker (1937) gives the following village names:

On Rogue River:

Gwi'sat huntun, on Mussel Creek near Sixes River and
sometimes separated as the Sixes tribe.

Kusu'me, on what is now called Flores Creek.

Kwataime, a short distance north of last.

Kwuse'tun, near and possibly a suburb of Megwino'tun, on the
coast.

Megwino'tun, a few miles up river.

Skame'me, between Pistol River and mouth of Rogue River;
Waterman places it at Hunter's Creek.

Sukwe'me or Sukwe'tce, at mouth of Sixes River.

Tagrili'tun, a suburb of Tu'tutun.

Tce'metun or Tce'me, really two towns, one on each side of the
river's mouth.

Tce'tlersh tcuntun, on Pistol River, perhaps belonging to the
Chetco.

Tu'tutun, 5 to 6 miles from the river's mouth, divided into two
parts called Tatre'tun, "downriver," and Na'gutretun
"upriver."

Yukwi'tce or Yu'gwitce, on what is now called Euchre Creek.

Berreman (1937) makes seven major divisions as follows:

Kwatami or Sixes River
Euchre Creek (Yukichetunne)
Mikono tunne
Pistol River (Chetleschantunne)
Joshua
Tututunne, (Tututni)
Kwaishtunne or Khustenete

History: A system prevailed among the men to never
marry within their own villages and any children would
belong to the village of the father. Each village seemed
unique, though within the tribe, for the villages often waged
war against one another.

An official report of Elijah H. Meservey, Captain of

Volunteers, has been located in Oregon State Archives and a copy sent to the Curry County Historical Society in Gold Beach. Some quotations from the report notes the men were called the "Gold Beach Guards," and appears to reflect the attitude of whites concerning the Indians. The Guard was made up of 21 men, mostly itinerant miners, formed to protect miners and settlers from remnants of the Rogue River Indians which had escaped the roundup of Indians destined for the Grande Ronde Reservation. Captain Meservey reported horses being stolen, as well as equipment, while the men were in the field, then the Indians destroying the camp while the men were evidently on patrol. On July 2, 1858, the day the unit was mustered out of the service, Captain Meservey reported to the State Adjutant General, "The last red men have been captured and shot, only women and children spared and they are enroute to the reserv[ation]. All further apprehension of danger is at an end and this portion of Oregon will rest in tranquility."

Population:

```
1854   1,311
1910     383 (U.S. Census)
1930      41 (B.I.A.)
          55 (under Megwino'tum)
          45 (under Joshua Tcemetum)
```

Tyigh

Various spellings: Attayes, Iyich, Ta-ih, Thy, Tyh, Tygh.

Also called:

Teáxtkni (Télknikni), Klamath name
Tse Amínema, Luckiamute Kalapuya name.

Linguistic group: Shapwailutan, Tenino branch of Shahaptian division

Location: on the eastern foothills of Cascade Mountains in region of Tygh and White Rivers. (See Tenino)

History: The Tyigh took part in the 1855 Wasco Treaty of 1855 and were sent to the Warm Springs Reservation.

Population:

```
1854   500 (Swanton)
1859   450 (Swanton)
1910   550 (U.S. Census, includes others on
             Warm Springs Reservation)
```

Names by which remembered: Tygh Creek, town (ZIP 97063); valley, ridge (over 3,000 ft. elev.).

Umatilla
Also called:

> Youmalolam, by Lewis and Clark
> You-matella, by Alexander Ross (Umatallow)
> Utalla, Townsend (Ewmitilly)
> Eu-o-tal-la, by Irving.

Linguistic group: Shapwailutan, Shahaptian dialect
Location: Along the Umatilla River and on its mouth with the Columbia River.
History: These Indians seem to be remnants from tribes after the extermination of many Cayuses and Walla Wallas. The name's origin is in doubt and may have been the brainchild of Lewis and Clark. One puzzlement is that the dialect of this group is significantly distinct from that of the Walla Wallas. In 1855 these Indians were a part of the treaty with the United States and were sent to the Umatilla Reservation which is east of Pendleton.
Population:

```
1780   1,500 (with Walla Wallas—Mooney, 1928)
1905     250 (with others)
1910     272 (U.S. Census)
1923     145 (B.I.A.)
1937     124 (B.I.A.)
1950   1,150 (Yenne)
1985   1,578 (Umatilla Reservation)
1987   (See Appendix)
```

Names by which remembered: A reservation; river; county; city (ZIP 97882); national forest.

Umpqua
Also called:

>
> Amgútsuish, Shasta name.
> Cacta^n'-qwût-me'tûnne, Naltunne name.
> Ci-cta'-qwût-me'tûnne, Tutuni name, meaning "Umpqua River people."
> Ci-sta'-qwût, Chastacosta name.
> Etnémitane, own name.
> Tsan Ampkua amím, Luckiamute Kalapuya name, meaning "people on the Umpqua.'
> Upper Umpqua.
> Ya^{n}galá, Takelma name.

Linguistic group: Athapascan
Location: Upper Umpqua River east of Kuitsh.

Subdivisions: The Umpqua on Cow Creek are often spoken of separately under the name Nahankhuotana. Parker (1840) mentions a people called Palakahu which was probably and Athapascan or Yakonan tribe but cannot now be identified, and also the Skoton and Chasta, probably parts of the Chastacosta or Tututni. This is all the more likely as he includes the Kwatami band of the Tututni and the entirely independent Chilula of California. Their chief village was Hewut.

History: Students of the Umpqua believe the tribe once numbered around 400, probably between 1845-1850 having been larger but reduced by disease. Hodge points out that at one time all Athapascan tribes were considered divisions of the Umpqua. One spelling being Umptqua, and Alexander Ross called the tribe Imp-qua. The remnants of the tribe were marched to the Grande Ronde Reservation.

Population:

>
> 1846   400 (Hale)
> 1902   84 (Grande Ronde Reservation)
> 1910   109 (U.S. Census)
> 1937   43 (B.I.A.)
> 1987 (See Appendix)

Names by which remembered: A river; town (ZIP

97486); major Coast Guard lighthouse; state park; community college.

Walla Walla (Wallawalla)

Although primarily found in Washington, this tribe visited Oregon (State) on hunting expeditions. (See Washington)

Walpapi

Commonly called Snake Indians, associated with Northern Paiute. (See Nevada)

Waluga

For some years there have been inquiries about the "Waluga Indians"; however, the word "Waluga" is merely an Indian word for a "white swan," according to McArthur.

Warm Springs (See Tenino)

Wasco

The name is from a Wasco word "wacq!ó" meaning "cup or small bowl [made] of horn." This reference is on account of a cup-shaped rock close to the main village of the Wascos. Taken from tribal name "Galasq!ó" meaning "those that belong to Wasco" or "those who have the cup." Hodge declares that the Wasco name from the Shahaptian "wask!ú," meaning "grass" "lacks probability."

Also called:

> Afúlakin, by the Kalapuya.
> Amp χänkni, meaning "where the water is," by the Klamath.
> Awásko ammim, by the Kalapuya.
> Sá χlatks, by the Molalla.

Linguistic group: Chinookian, with close relatives being the Wishram on the north side of the Columbia River. Wasco and Wishram appear to be the farthest east of the

Oregon

Chinookian group.

Location: Vicinity of The Dalles in present Wasco
County, Oregon.

Villages and fishing locations: From east to west
(downstream on Columbia River):

Hlgahacha	Hlilwaihldik
Igiskhis	Hliapkenum
Wasco (upstream a few miles	Kabala
from city of The Dalles)	Gayahisitik
Wogupan	Itkumahlemkt
Natlalaik	Higaktahlk
Gawobumat	Igahu
Hliekals-imadik	Hliluktik
Wikatk	Gahlentlich
Watsokus	Gechgechak
Winkwot (at The Dalles)	Skhlalis

History: The Wasco used several villages, as identified,
as well as seasonal fishing stations. This tribe was primarily
sedentary and lived off fish, which was available for the
taking year-around. While they gathered edible roots and
berries, they did not often go on hunts for game. Salmon
were caught in the spring and fall, partly with dip-nets,
partly by spearing; smaller fish were obtained with hook
and line or by means of basket traps. Definitely located
fishing stations were a well-recognized form of personal
property; the capture of the first salmon of the season was
accompanied with a ceremony intended to give that
particular fishing station a good season's catch. Pounded
salmon flesh was often stored away for winter use; it also
formed an important article of trade with neighboring
tribes, the chief rendezvous for barter being the falls a few
miles above The Dalles. Also berries were dried and
preserved for winter use. The most notable of their
industries were works in wood, making spoons and bowls.
With horns (but no source for horn is mentioned) they made
spoons and cups. The Wasco were quite proficient makers
of twined baskets, mostly stiff baskets for carrying loads,
usually fish from the river to the villages.

Coiled basketry was learned from their contact with the

111

Klickitat. The twining was done with cedar roots and grasses, then later with cord and yarn received from traders.

The original Wasco costume consisted of blanket robes (the pelts of bear, deer, wolf, coyote, raccoon, and mountain goat in summer), sleeveless shirts of raccoon or coyote skin, breechcloths of raccoon skin, and moccasins of deerskin; hats and gloves were made of coyote skin. Two types of houses were in use—the partly underground winter house, roofed with cedar bark and having board platforms about the walls for beds, and the summer house with frame of fir poles and covering of tules or cedar bark; the latter type might have several fireplaces, accommodating three or four families. Sweat-houses were frequently used and were of quasi-supernatural significance.

In childhood the head was flattened by pressure on the forehead, and the ears were punctured with five holes in each ear; adults whose heads were not flattened were derided as no better than slaves. As regards naming, the most interesting fact is perhaps the absolute impossibility of translating a single Wasco name, the Chinookian dialects differing in this respect from the vast majority of American languages.

Puberty ceremonies were observed in the case of both girls and boys. The former were subject to the usual taboos, after the fulfilment of which a menstrual dance was held, while the latter "trained" for the acquirement of strength and one or several guardian spirits.

Burial was on boards put away in "dead people's houses." Slaves were sometimes buried alive to accompany a chief to the next world.

Three classes of society were recognized: chiefs (the chieftainship was hereditary), common folk, and slaves (obtained by capture). There was no clan or totem organization, the guardian spirits referred to being strictly personal in character; the village was the main social unit. Religious ideas centered in the acquirement and manifestation of supernatural power obtained from one or more guardian spirits. The main social dances were the menstrual dance, the guardian spirit dance, in which each participant sang a song that nad been revealed by one's protector, and the scalp dance. The most exciting factor in the legends of the Wasco was the great role of Coyote as culture-hero and transformer. The tribe moved to Warm Springs Reservation following the 1855 treaty.

Population:

```
1822   900 (Morse)
1910   242 (U.S. Census)
1937   227 (B.I.A.)
```

Names by which remembered: Wasco Indians were the strongest warriors of the Upper Chinooks thus ultimately absorbed the rest. The name is preserved by name of a county; a town (ZIP 97055); towns in California and in Illinois.

Watlala

Also called:

Cascade Indians, the popular English name.
Gila'xicatck, by the Chinook.
Katlagakya, own name.
Shahala, from Chinook saxala, meaning "above," by Chinook.

Linguistic group: Chinookian, Clackamas dialect
Location: Villages extended on the Columbia River from the cascades of the river to mouth of Willamette River. Observe one village on north side of river at Washougal.

Subdivisions: The following names have been applied by various writers to the Indians in this neighborhood and may be subdivisions of this tribe, or perhaps refer to the entire tribe itself:

Cathlakaheckit, at the Cascades.
Cathlathlala, just below the Cascades.
Clahclellah, near the foot of the Cascades.
Neerchokioon, on the south side of Columbia River a few miles above Sauvie Island.
Washougal, near Washougal River.
Yehuh, just above the Cascades.

History: Early writers include several tribes at or near the cascades and at least in later times on Dog (Hood) River, but as the population along the Columbia River was very changeable because it was such a desirable fishing stream, intermingling was bound to occur. Many of the so-called tribes were often just villages, some quite small, thus traders, trappers and opportunists traveling through the area were likely to record these Indians in different manners.

Following the epidemic of 1829, the Watlala seem to have been the only remaining tribe, the remnants of the others having probably united under that name, though they were commonly called Cascade Indians by whites.

In 1855 the Watlala took part in the Wasco treaty under the name, "Ki-gal-twal-la band of the Wasco" and the "Dog River band of Wasco" then were moved to Warm Springs Reservation.

The term Watlala is also used by some writers, following Hale, to include all the Upper Chinook, the name given by different writers to the tribes living at or near the cascades.

Population:

1780	3,200 (Mooney, 1928)
1805-06	2,800 (Lewis and Clark)
1812	1,400 (Swanton)
1854	80 (Hodge—probably low)

Since 1854 not enumerated separately, but probably included with Wasco.

Yahuskin (Northern Paiute. See Nevada)

Yamel
Sometimes spelled Yam Hill.
Also called:

Ycha-yamel-amin, by the Atfalati Kalapuya.

Linguistic group: Kalapooian, northern dialect division

Location: Yamhill River.
Subdivisions:

Andshankualth, on a western tributary of the Willamette.
Andshimmampak, on Yamhill River.
Chamifu, in the forks of Yamhill River.
Chamiwi, on Yamhill River.
Champikle, on Dallas (La Creole) Creek.
Chinchal, on Dallas Creek.

Population:

1910   5 (U.S. Census)

Names by which remembered: A county; city (ZIP 97148); river.

Yaquina
Also called:

Iakon or Yakone
Youikeones, by Lewis and Clark
Youkone
Yacone
Acoma
Sa-ákl, Nestucca name
Sis'-qûn-me'tûnne, Chetco name
Tcha yákon amim, Luckiamute Kalapuya name.

Linguistic group: Yakonan
Villages:

On the north side of Yaquina River:

Holukhik	Mittsulstik
Hunkkhwitik	Shash
Iwai	Thlalkhaiuntik
Khaishuk	Thlekakhaik
Khilukh	Tkhakiyu
Kunnupiyu	Tshkitshiauk
Kwulaishauik	Tthilkitik
Kyaukuhu	Ukhwaiksh
Kyuwatkal	Yahal
Mipshuntik	Yikkhaich

On the south side of the river:

Atshuk	Kwullakhtauik
Chulithltiyu	Kwutichuntthe
Hakkyaiwal	Mulshintik
Hathletukhish	Naaish
Hitshinsuwit	Paiinkhwutthu
Hiwaitthe	Pikiiltthe
Kaku	Pkhulluwaaitthe
Khaiyukkhai	Pkuuniukhtauk
Khitalaitthe	Puuntthiwaun
Kholkh	Shilkhotshi
Khulhanshtauk	Shupauk
Kilauutuksh	Thlekwiyauik
Kumsukwum	Thlelkhus
Kutshuwitthe	Thlinaitshtik
Kwaitshi	Thlukwiutshthu
Kwilaishauk	Tkulmashaauk
Kwulchichicheshk	Tuhaushuwitthe
Kwullaish	Tulshk

Location: Along Yaquina River and its bay.

History: The tribe, always small, appeared to be nearly gone by 1905. What few survivors were of mixed blood and were on the Siletz Reservation.

Population:

1910   19 (U.S. Census)

Names by which remembered: Yaquina River; bay; town (post office 1868-1961); Yaquina John Point on south side of entrance to Alsea Bay; major Coast Guard station; lighthouse.

Yoncalla (Yonkalla)
Also called:

Tch'Ayanke'ld ("those living at Ayankeld"—their own name).

Linguistic group: Kalapooian. Southernmost tribe of the group.

Location: On Elk and Calapooya creeks, part of Umpqua River drainage.

Subdivisions:

Chayankeld/Tsantokayu, by the Luckiamutes.

History: Hodge, in his paper in 1905, remarks that at that time the Yoncallas were "probably extinct," however the U.S. Census reported a total of 11 in 1910.

Names by which remembered: Valley in Douglas County; a mountain; city (ZIP 97499).

CHAPTER 5

WASHINGTON

Calasthocle (See Quinault)

Calispel (See Kalispel)

Cathlamet
Also called (and spelled):

> Cathlamah
> Kathlamet (own name)
> Katalamet
> Kahelamit
> Guasámas (or Guthlamethl) by the Clackamas
> Kwillu'chini

Linguistic group: Chinookian. This dialect is used as far upstream of the Columbia River as Oak Point on the Washington side, and Rainier on the Oregon side.

Location: Along the south bank of the Columbia from Tongue Point to Puget Island as well as along the north bank from Grays Bay to an undetermined location probably midway between Oak Point and Longview.

Villages:

> Ika'naiak, on the north side of the Columbia River at the mouth of Coal Creek Slough just east of Oak Point.
> Ilo'humin, on the north side of Columbia River opposite Puget Island and near the mouth of Alockman Creek.
> Kathla'amat, on the south side of Columbia River about four miles below Puget Island.
> Ta'nas ilu', on Tanas Ilahee Island on the south side of the Columbia River.
> Wa'kaiyakam, across Alockman Creek opposite Ilo'humin.

Population:

1780   450 (Mooney, 1928)
1805-06   300 (Lewis and Clark)
1849   58 (Hodge)
Reported extinct by Swanton in 1952.

Names by which remembered: City (ZIP 98612); channel in the Columbia River.

Cathlapotle

("People of the Na p̓!olx (Lewis) River"
Linguistic group: Chinookian
Location: In Clark County on the lower Lewis River and in at least one location on the Columbia River.
Villages:

> The main village of the Cathlapotle was Nahpooitle, at the mouth of Lewis River, but to this should perhaps be added Wakanasisi, opposite the mouth of Willamette River.

Population:

1780   1,300
1806   900 (Lewis and Clark)

Names by which remembered: Cathlapotle (Cathlapootie) River was an earlier name for the Lewis River.

Cayuse

The Cayuse gained national recognition with their massacre of Dr. and Mrs. Marcus Whitman, and others, at Waiilatpu in November 1847. (See Oregon)

Chehalis

Also called:

> Chi-ke-lis ("shifting sands")
> Atchi χe'lish, Calapooya name.
> Ilga't, Nestucca name.
> Lower Chehalis, name used by Spier (1927).
> Staq-tûbe, Puyallup name.

Linguistic group: Salishan, coastal division with closest

119

relatives being Humptulips, Quinault and Wynoochee.

Location: Along the lower Chehalis River, mostly on the south side as well as along the south shore of Grays Harbor. In more recent times the tribe occupied former Chinook territory at Willapa Bay.

Villages:

> Chehalis (Gibbs, 1877), on the south side of Grays Harbor near Westport, in country earlier occupied by the Chinook.
> Chiklisilkh (Gibbss), at Point Ledbetter, Willapa Bay, earlier occupied by Chinook.
> Hlakwun (Curtis, 1907-9), near Willapa on Willapa river, earlier occupied by the Chinook.
> Kaulhlak (Curtis), at the head of Palux River, earlier in Chinook country.
> Klumaitumsh (Biggs and Boas personal information), given doubtfully as the name of a former band or village on the south side of Grays Harbor at its entrance.
> Nai'yasap (Curtis), on Willapa River earlier occupied by Chinook
> Nickomin (Swan, 1857 and Boas, personal information), on North River which flows into Willapa Bay, earlier occupied by Chinook.
> Noohooultch (Gibbs), on the south side of Grays Harbor.
> Noosiatsks (Gibbs), on the south side of Grays Harbor.
> Nooskoh (Gibbs), on a creek opposite Whishkah River.
> Qyan (Gairdner, 1841), on the north point of Grays Harbor.
> Talal (Gibbs), at Ford's Prairie on the Chehalis River near Centralia, and therefore far outside of the Chehalis territory proper.
> Willapa, on Willapa River in earlier Chinook country.

The following villages were originally occupied by Chinook but seem to have shifted in population or language or both so as to become Chehalis:

Hwa'hots	Quer'quelin
Nutskwethlso'k	Tske'lsos
Quela'ptonlilt	

History: There was an epidemic of some great proportions in 1829 which apparently wiped out many Chinooks, thus the remnants of Chinooks, according to Yenne, joined

the Chehalis and adopted their language. Tribe moved to
Chehalis Reservation.
Population:

1780	1,000 (Mooney, 1928; combines Lower and Upper Chehalis, Cowlitz, Humptulips and plausibly the Satsop)
1907	170 (Swanton)
1910	282 (U.S. Census—Cowlitz excluded)
1923	89 (B.I.A.)
1937	131 (B.I.A.)
1985	777 (Reservation)
1987	(See Appendix)

Names by which remembered: River; county; city (ZIP
98532); reservation.

Chelan

Linguistic group: Salishan, Wenatchee dialect
Location: At confluence of Chelan and Columbia River
primarily on the Chelan River.
Population: No data available.
Names by which remembered: A river; village (ZIP
98817); city (ZIP 98816); mountains; national forest.

Chilluckittequaw

Linguistic group: Chinookian
Location: Lewis and Clark reported this tribe along the
north shore of the Columbia River in present Skamania and
Klickitat Counties from about ten miles below The Dalles
extending downstream to the Cascades. One researcher
believed the tribe crossed the Columbia River and in fact
were the same as Indians in the Hood River area (Spier,
1936), however there is no mention of this in Hood River
area tribe (see Watlala in Oregon).
Subdivisions and villages:

Itkilak or Ithlkilak (occupied jointly with Klickitat), at White
Salmon Landing.
Nanshuit (occupied jointly with Klickitat), at the present
Underwood (ZIP 98651).

Smackshop, a band extending from the River Labiche (Hood River?) to the Cascades.

Tgasgutcu (occupied jointly with Klickitat), said to be about ½ mile west of a long, high mountain opposite Mosier, Oreg., and at the same time about a mile above White Salmon Landing, an apparent inconsistency.

Thlmieksok or Thlmuyaksok, ½ mile from the last; in 1905 the site of the Burket Ranch.

History: Mooney reported (1928) a remnant of this tribe lived near mouth of White Salmon River until 1880 then moved to the Cascades where he reported a few in 1895.

Population:

1780   3,000 (Mooney, 1928)
1806   1,400 (Lewis and Clark)
          + 800 (Lewis and Clark, on Oregon side)

Chimakum (Chimacum)
Also called:

Aqokúlo, their own name
Port Townsend Indians, the popular name

Linguistic group: Chimakum. Was composed of Chimakum Hoh and Quileute and may have been connected with Salishan group.

Location: On peninsula from Port Townsend south and extending into Hood Canal across from Seabeck.

History: This tribe was constantly warring with the Clallam and other Salish tribes. Being small in number they suffered heavily. Chimakum were a part of the Point-no-Point Treaty in 1855 then moved to the Skokomish Reservation. In reservation life their numbers further diminished until Boas, in 1850, could locate only three persons who spoke the language and at that imperfectly.

Population:

1780   400 (Mooney, 1928)
1855   90 (Gibbs)
1910   3 (U.S. Census)

Washington

Names and reasons remembered: Uniqueness of language and war-like character; valley; city (ZIP 98325); creek.

Chinook
Also called:

> Tsinúk, Chelalis name
> Ala'dshtish, Nestucca name
> Flatheads, because the purposefully deformed their heads
> Thlál'h, Clackamasɪ name

Linguistic group: Chinookian, lower Chinook division
Location: Along the north side of the Columbia River from mouth (Ilwaco) to Grays Bay (near Altoona)—do not confuse with Grays Harbor—about 15 miles then north along the ocean frontage to include Willapa Bay.
Villages:

> Clamoitomish (Sapir, 1930), in Grays Bay.
> Hakelsh, at the mouth of Smith Creek on the northeast shore of Willapa Bay.
> (Wharhoots), a settlement at Bruceport (post office 1858-1879) about three miles north of mouth of Palix River, five miles west of South Bend (ZIP 98586).
> Ini'sal, on Naselle river where it enters the arm of Willapa Bay.
> Iwa'lhat, at the mouth of Wallicut River, which bears its name in a corrupted form.
> Kalawa'uus, on the peninsula at Oysterville Point.
> Killaxthokle (Lewis and Clark, 1905-6), probably on Willapa Bay.
> Kwatsa'mts, on Baker Bay at the mouth of Chinook River.
> Lapi'lso, on an island in an arm of Willapa Bay below the mouth of Naselle River.
> Ma'hu, at the mouth of Nemah River below Nemah (post office 1894-1923).
> Mo'kwal, at the mouth of Deep River on Grays Bay.
> Nahume'nsh, on the west side of North River at its mouth on the north shore of Willapa Bay.
> Namla'iks, at Goose Point.
> Na'mstcats, at a site called Georgetown between Tokeland and North Cove.
> (Note: North Cove no longer exists, having been totally

123

inundated due to coastal erosion which ate away the entire Cape Shoalwater by 1983. North Cove was a nicely sheltered cove on the east side of the cape. The area of the cove was gone by 1921. In 1989 the remainder of the shoreline west of Tokeland is locally called "Wash-away Beach." For losses by erosion along coastal Oregon and Washington, refer to the editor's book *Maimed by the Sea*.)

Nokska'itmithls, at Fort Canby on Cape Disappointment.

No'skwalakuthl, at Ilwaco, named after its last chief.

Nu'kaunthl, at Tokeland, named after its chief.

Nu'patstcthl, at the site of Nahcotta (ZIP 98637) opposite mouth of Nemah River.

Nutskwethlso'k, on Willapa Bay west of Bay Center (ZIP 98527).

Nuwi'lus, on the site of Grayland (ZIP 98547).

Quela'ptonlilt (Swan, 1857), at the mouth of Willapa River.

Querquelin (Swan), at the mouth of Querquelin River, which flows into Palix River from the south near the mouth of the latter.

Se'akwal, on the north bank of the Columbia a short distance below Mo'kwal.

Tokpi'luks, at the mouth of Palix River.

Tse'yuk, at Oysterville (ZIP 98641).

Tske'lsos, on Willapa River between South Bend and Raymond.

Ya'kamnok, at Sandy Point three miles south of Goose Point, the extreme north point at Bay Center.

History: The Chinook had been known to traders for an indefinite period previously, but were first described by Lewis and Clark, who visited them in 1805. From their proximity to Astoria and their intimate relations with early traders, they soon became well known. Their language formed the chief Indian basis for the Chinook jargon, first employed as a trade language, which ultimately extended from California to Alaska. In the middle of the nineteenth century, the Chinook became mixed with the Chehalis with whom they ultimately fused entirely, dropping their own language. The Chinook of later census returns are composed of a number of tribes of the same stock.

Population:

1780   800 (Mooney, 1928)

1805	400 (Lewis and Clark count of just those on Columbia River)
1885	112 (Swan—probably limited to Columbia River region. There were 500 on reservations)
1931	3 (Ray, 1936)

Names by which remembered: Name became famous due to intermingling and dealings with American and British traders; their names used to class linguistic group; their name used to identify the jargon (Oregon Trade Language) used throughout the Pacific Northwest; name for Pacific trade wind, the "Chinook" wind; town in Washington (ZIP 98641); in Montana (ZIP 59523); creek; mountain pass; Chinook Point (navigation); river.

Some examples of Chinook Jargon:

Able—*skookum.*
Aborigines—*siwash.*
Above—*saghalie.*
Act, action—*mamook.*
Afraid—*kwass.*
Ah! (in pain)—*anah.*
Alarm—*mamook kwass.*
Almighty, The—*Saghalie Tyee.*
And—*pe.*
Anger, angry—*solleks.*
Argue—*hiyu wawa.*
Arrive, arrive at—*ko; chako; klap.*
Arrow—*kalitan; stick lakitan.*
Ask—*wawa.*
Axe—*lahash.*
Baby—*tenas.*
Bad—*mesachchie; peshak; cultus.*
Bargain—*mahkook; huyhuy.*
Bark—*stickskin.*
Basket—*opekwan; basket.*
Battle—*pight.*
Beads—*kamosuk.*
Bear (black)—*itchwoot; chetwoot; itswoot.*
Bed—*bed.*
Beg—*skookum wawa.*
Belly—*yakwahtin.*
Beyond—*yahwa.*

Big—*has.*
Bird—*kallakala; kulakula.*
Blackberries—*klale olallie; klikamuks.*
Blanket—*pasesse.*
Blood—*pilpil*
Boat—*boat.*
Bowl—*la casett; la kassett.*
Boy—*tenas man.*
Bread—*le pan; sapolil; piah sopolil.*
Breasts—*tatoosh.*
Breath—*wind.*
Brother—*ow.*
Bucket—*tamolitsh.*
Buffalo—*moosmoos; wild moosmoos.*
Bury—*mahsh kopa illahee.*
By-and-by—*winapie; alki.*
Can—*skookum kopa.*
Cannot—*halo skookum kopa; howkutl.*
Canoe—*canim.*
Cap—*seahpo.*
Captive—*elite.*
Cash—*dolla; chikamin.*
Cattle—*moosmoos.*
Chief—*tyee.*
Child—*tenas.*
Clams (one)—*lukutchee; lakwitchee.*
Clothes—*iktas.*
Clouds—*smoke; smoke kopa saghalie; cultus smoke.*
Coast—*illahee wake siah kopa chuck.*
Coat—*capo; kapo.*
Cold—*cole.*
Cook—*mamook piah; mamook piah muckamuck.*
Cost (how much?)—*kunsih dolla?*
Coyote—*talapus.*
Curse (v.)—*wawa mesachie.*
Dance to—*tanse.*
Daughter—*tenas klootchman.*
Dead—*memaloose; mahsh konaway yaka wind.*
Demon—*skookum; lejaub; kahkwa lejaub.*
Dig a hole—*mamook hole; mamook tlwhop.*
Dishonest—*kumtux kapswalla.*
Doctor—*doctin.*
Dog—*kahmooks.*
Dollar—*dolla; tahla; chickamin.*
Dress—*klootchman coat.*
Drink, to—*muckamuck; muckamuck chuck; kaupy.*

126

Drum (Indian)—*pompon.*
Drunk (adj.)—*pahtlum dlunk.*
Ear—*kwolann.*
Earth—*illahee.*
Egg—*lesap; lesap; hen olallie.*
Elk—*moolock; mooluk.*
End—*opoots.*
England—*King George Illahee.*
English, Englishman—*King Chautsh; King George tillikum.*
Excuse—*mamook klahowya.*
Eye, eyeball—*seeowist.*
Face—*seeowist.*
False, falsehood—*kliminawhit; tseepie.*
Fat—*glease.*
Father—*papa.*
Feast—*muckamuck; hiyu muckamuck.*
Female—*klootchman.*
Fight, to—*mamook solleks; pight; mamook pukpuk.*
Fingers—*le doo; lemah.*
Fire—*piah; olapitski.*
Fish—*pish.*
Fog—*smoke; cultus smoke.*
Food—*muckamuck.*
Foot—*lepee.*
Footsteps, footprints—*kah leepee mitlite.*
Fox—*talapus; hyas opoots talapus.*
Friend—*sikhs tillikum.*
Fuel—*piah stick.*
Full—*pahtl.*
Gamble—*gamble; mamook gamble; mamook itlokum; heehee
    lemah* (with disks) *chis chis; itlokum.*
Get out—*klatawa; mahsh.*
Ghost—*tahmahnawis; skookum.*
Gift—*cultus potlatch.*
Gun—*musket; sukwalal.*
Gunpowder—*polallie.*
Head—*la tet.*
Heart—*tumtum.*
Help, to—*mamook elann; mamook help.*
Honest—*wake kapswalla; halo kumtux kapswalla.*
Horse—*kuitan.*
Hostile—*solleks.*
Hot—*hyas waum.*
House—*house.*
How are you—*klahowya.*
I—*nika.*

If—*spose.*
Indian—*siwash.*
Indian medicine—*kelale.*
Jail—*skookum house.*
Jargon (Chinook)—*Chinook.*
Job—*mamook.*
Kamass root—*lakamass.*
Kettle—*ketling.*
Kill—*mamook memaloose.*
Knife—*opitsah.*
Knot—*lemah; lemah kopa stick.*
Lazy—*lazy.*
Leg—*teahwhit; lepee.*
Lips—*lapush* (point to them)
Little—*tenas.*
Long ago—*ahnkuttie.*
Love, to—*ticky.*
Mad—*solleks.*
Maize—*corn; esalth.*
Man—*man.*
Market—*mahkook house.*
Massacre (v.)—*cultus mamook memoloose.*
Me—*nika.*
Merchandise—*iktas.*
Merchant—*mahkook man.*
Misconduct—*mesachie mamook.*
Misunderstand—*halo kumtux.*
Moccasins—*skin-shoes.*
Money—*chikamin; dolla.*
Moon—*moon.*
Mosquito—*melakwa; dago.*
Most—*elip hiyu kopa konaway.*
Mountain—*la monti; stone illahee; lamotai.*
Mouth—*la push; la boos.*
My, mine—*nika; kopa nika; nikas.*
Name—*nem; yahhul.*
Near—*wake siah.*
Neck—*le cou; lecoo.*
Needle—*keepwot; tupshin.*
Never—*wake kunsih.*
No, not—*halo; wake.*
Noisy—*hiyu noise.*
Noon—*sitkum sun.*
North—*kah cole chako.*
Nose—*nose; emeets.*
Numerals—

1. *ikt; icht.*
2. *mokst; moxt.*
3. *klone.*
4. *lakit; lokit.*
5. *kwinnim.*
6. *taghum; tughum.*
7. *sinamokst; sinamoxt.*
8. *stotekin.*
9. *kwaist; kweest.*
10. *tahtlum.*
100. *ikt takamonuk; icht tukamonuk; tahtlum-tahtlum,* ten tens.

Ocean—*hyas salt chuck.*
Off—*kitk.*
Open—*kahlakl; halakl.*
Overcoat—*hyas kapo.*
Owl—*waugh waugh; kwel kwel.*
Paddle (n.)—*isick.*
Pencil—*pencil; tzum stick.*
People—*tillikum; tillikums.*
Perspiration—*chuck mitlite kopa skin.*
Pig—*cosho; tenas cosho.*
Pine—*lagome stick.*
Pipe—*la peep; pipe.*
Pole—*la pehsh; pole.*
Pond—*memaloose chuck.*
Potato—*wappato; lapatak.*
President—*tyee kopa Washington* (Chief at Washington).
Prisoner—*tillikum kopa skookum house.*
Puke—*muckamuck yaka kilapie; kilapie muckamuck; mahsh yaka muckamuck klahanie kopa yaka lapush.*
Purchase—*mahkook.*
Quail (n.)—*illahee; kulakala.*
Questions—*wawa.*
Quiver—*stick kalitan lesak.*
Rabbit—*kwitshadie; kwitshoddle.*
Rain—*snass.*
Rat—*hyas hoolhool; colecole.*
Raven—*kaka* (caw caw).
Razor, knife—*opitsah.*
Remedy (v.)—*mamook kloshe.*
Remember (not to forget)—*mitlite kopa tumtum; wake kopet kumtux.*
Reply—*killapie wawa.*
Rest—*cultus mitlite.*
River—*chuck; cooley chuck; liver.*

129

Road—*ooahut; wayhut.*
Root—*stick keekwulee kopa illahee.*
Rope—*lope.*
Sad—*sick tumtum.*
Saddle—*la sell.*
Sailor—*shipman.*
Salmon—*salmon.*
Salt—*salt.*
Sand—*polallie; polallie illahee; tenas stone kahkwa polallie.*
Sea—*salt chuck; sea.*
Sheep—*lemoto.*
Shell money—(the small size) *coopcoop; allekacheek.* (the large)
    hykwa; haikwa.
Ship—*ship.*
Shirt—*shut.*
Shoal—*wake keekwulee.*
Shoes—*shoes; shush; tikitlipa.*
Shoot, to—*mamook poo.*
Shore—*illahee.*
Sick—*etsitsa.*
Silver—*tkope chikamin; tkope dolla.*
Skin—*skin.*
Sky—*koosagh; saghalie; ekusah.*
Slave—*elite; mistchimas; mistshimus.*
Sleep—*moosum; sleep.*
Smoke (n.)—*smoke.*
Snake—*oluk; wahpoos; snake.*
Snare, trap—*lapeage; kwalta.*
Snow—*snow; cole snass.*
Soap—*soap.*
Soldiers—*sogers.*
Spoon—*spoon.*
Steal, to—*kapswalla.*
Steamer—*piah ship; steamer; steamboat.*
Stone—*stone.*
Stop, to (imp.)—*kopet.*
Storm—(wind) *hiyu wind;* (rain) *hiyu snass.*
Strong—*skookum.*
Sun—*sun, otelagh.*
Sunday—*Sunday; Sante.*
Sunlight—*sun yaka light.*
Sunrise—*tenas sun; get up sun.*
Sunset—*tenas polaklie; klip sun.*
Survivor—*man halo memaloose.*
Tail—*opoots.*
Take off, or take out—*mamook haul; mamook klah; mamook
    klak; mahsh.*

Talk—*wawa.*
Tambourine or Indian drum—*pompom.*
Teeth—*la tah.*
Thirsty—*olo kopa chuck.*
Thread—*klapite; hwilom.*
Timber—*stick.*
Tobacco—*bacca; kinootl; kinoos; kimoolth.*
Today—*okoke sun.*
Tomorrow—*tomolla.*
Tongue—*la lang.*
Tonight—*okoke polaklie.*
Trade—*huyhuy.*
Tradesman—*mahkook man.*
Trail—*ooahu; tenas ooahut.*
Tree—*stick.*
Tribe—*lalang.*
Under—*keekwulee; keekwillie.*
Understand—*kumtux.*
Unhappy—*sick tumtum.*
Up—*saghalie.*
Utensil—*ikta.*
Vegetables—*konoway muckamuck chako kopa illahee.*
Venison—*mowitch.*
Violent—*skookum.*
Voyage—*klatawa kopa boat or ship.*
Wade—*klatawa kopa lapea kopa chuck.*
Walk—*klatawa kopa lapea.*
Warrior—*sogers; pight tillikum.*
Water—*chuck.*
We—*nesika.*
Wet—*pahtl chuck; chuck mitlite.*
West—*kah sun klatawa.*
Wheel—*chikchik; tsiktsik.*
Whiskey—*whiskey; lum.*
White—*tkope.*
Wife—*klootchman; oquackakull.*
Wild onions—*kalaka.*
Winter—*cole illahee.*
Wolf—*leloo; wolf.*
Woman—*klootchman.*
Wrong—*wake kloshe.*
Yankee—*Boston man.*
Year—*ikt cole.*
Yes—*nowitka; ahha.*
Yesterday—*tahlkie sun.*
You, your (if singular)—*mika.*
You, your (if plural)—*mesika.*

Clackama (Clackamas)
Historical research indicates this tribe lived on both sides of the Columbia River, however more contemporary studies indicate if this was so, the major bands were on the south side of the river, particularly along the Clackamas River and at the confluence with the Willamette River. (See Oregon)

Clallam
Also called:

> Nu-sklaim; S'Klallam (their own name)
> Callam
> Kla-kla-wice
> Do-sklal-ob (Twana) "big strong nation (or people)."

Linguistic group: Salishan
Location: Along the south shore of Strait of Juan de Fuca between Port Discovery and Hoko River at Sekiu. Later, the tribe occupied former Chimakum territory most likely near Port Townsend, and some were noted on the southern end of Vancouver Island.
Villages:

> Elwah, at mouth of Elwah River.
> Hoko, at mouth of Hoko River.
> Huiauulch, on site of Jamestown 3½ miles north of Sequim.
> Hunnint or Hungi'ngit, on the east side of Clallam Bay; this town and Klatlawas together were called Xainañt by Erna Gunther (1927).
> Kahtai, at Port Townsend, occupied after the destruction of the Chimakum.
> Kaquaith (or Skakwiyel), at Port Discovery. Klatlawas, the Tlatlawai'is of Curtis (1907-9), on the west side of Clallam Bay; see Hunnint.
> Kwahamish, a fishing village on the Lyre river.
> Mekoös, on Beecher Bay, Vancouver Island, B.C. Pistchin, on Pysht Bay.
> Sequim or Suktcikwii!n, on Sequim Bay or Washington Harbor.
> Sestietl, Upper Elwah.
> Stehtlum, at new Dungeness.
> Tclanuk, on Beecher Bay, Vancouver Island, B.C.

Tsako, at the former mouth of Dungeness River.
Tsewhizen, on Ediz Hook (earlier called Port Angeles Spit) between 2 and 3 miles west of ghost village of Stehtlum, probably near base of the hook.
Yennis, at Port Angeles (earlier called False Dungeness) was a fortified tribal village. Hitchman says "Yennis" means "good place."

Population:

1780	2,000 (Mooney, 1928)
1854	800 (Gibbs)
1855	926
1862	1,300 (Ells, an estimate)
1878	597 (Ells, estimate)
1881	485 (Ells, estimate)
1904	336 (Swanton)
1910	398 (U.S. Census)
1923	535 (B.I.A.)
1937	764 (B.I.A.)
1987	(See Appendix)

Names by which remembered: A bay; county; river; city (ZIP 98326); Clallam Point (navigation, now named Diamond Point in *U.S. Coast Pilot 7*).

Clalskanie (See Clatskanie—Oregon)

Columbia or Sinkiuse-Columbia

The latter because their former important association having most of their villages along the Columbia River.
Also called:

Botcaced, by the Nez Percé, probably meaning "arrows" or "arrow people."
Isle-de-Pierre, a trader's name, perhaps from a place in their country or for a band.
Middle Columbia Salish, so called by Teit (1928) and Spier (1930 b).
Papspê'lu, Nez Percé name, meaning "firs" or "fir-tree people."
Sa'ladebc, probably a Snohomish name.
Sinkiuse, the name applied to themselves and most other

neighboring Salish tribes, said to have belonged originally and properly to a band which once inhabited Umatilla Valley.

Suwa'dabc, Snohomish name for all interior Indians, meaning "inland people," or "interior people."

Swa'dab.c, Twana name for all interior Indians, meaning "inland people."

Swa'namc, Nootsak name for interior Indians, meaning "inland people."

Ti'attluxa, Wasco Chinook name.

Tskowa'xtsɛnux or .skowa'xtsɛnɛx, applied by themselves, meaning has something to do with "main valley."

Linguistic group: Salishan, inland division. Nearest relatives the Wenatchee and Methow.

Subdivisions:

Nkee'us or .s.nkeie'usox (Umatilla Valley).

Stata'ketux, around White Bluffs on the Columbia.

Tskowa'xtsɛnux or .skow'xtsɛnɛx, also called Moses-Columbia or Moses Band after a famous chief (Priest's Rapids and neighboring country).

Curtis (1907-9) gives the following: "Near the mouth of the sink of Crab Creek were the Sinkumkunatkuh, and above them the Sinkolkoluminuh. Then came in succession the Stapi'sknuh, the Skukulat'kuh, the Skoáhchnuh, the Skihikintnuh, and, finally, the Skultaqchi'mh, a little above the mouth of Wenatchee River." Spier (1927) adds that the Sinkowarsin met by Thompson in 1811 might have been a band of this tribe.

Location and history: The Sinkiuse-Columbia lived on the east side of Columbia River from Fort Okanogan to the neighborhood of Point Eaton. Later a reservation was created for them known as Columbia Reservation. In 1870 Winans placed them "on the east and south sides of the Columbia River from the Grand Coulée down to Priest's Rapids. In 1952 they were under the jurisdiction of Colville Agency and one band, the Moses-Columbia Band, was in the southern part of Spokane Reservation.

Population:

1780   800 (Mooney, 1928; but probably many

more as Teit [1927] links this tribe with
the Pisquow totaling about 10,000
before smallpox decimated them.)

1905   355 (Swanton)
1908   299 (Swanton)
1909   540 (presumed to include others—Swanton)
1910   52 (U.S. Census)

Names by which remembered: The name "Columbia" has been in general use countless numbers of places among which are these: a river; a barracks (Ft. Vancouver); Columbia Center in Garfield County; city (ZIP 98118); county; Columbia River (town, post office in Douglas County 1908-1926); and others.

Colville
The name originated from name of a post of the Hudson's Bay Company, Fort Colville, at Kettle Falls of the Columbia River, the fort being named for the governor of the company in London at the time the fort was established in 1825.

Also called:

> Basket People, by Hale (1846).
> Chaudière, French name derived from the popular term applied to them, Kettle Falls Indians.
> Kettle Falls Indians, as above.
> Sälsχuyilp, Okanogan name.
> Skuyélpi, by other Salish tribes.
> Whe-el-po, by Lewis and Clark.

Linguistic group: Salishan, inland division includes Okanogan, Sanpoil, Senjijextee.

Location: Along Colville River and along the Columbia River from Kettle Falls (ZIP 99141) downstream to Hunters (ZIP 99137). This area of the Columbia River is now Roosevelt Lake, slack water behind Grand Coulee Dam.

Subdivisions and villages:

> Kakalapia, home of Skakalapiak, across from former village of Harvey (post office 1887-1925).
> Kilumaak, home of the Skilumaak (opposite the present town of Kettle Falls, about 1½ miles above Nchumutastum).

Nchaliam, home of the Snchalik (about 1½ miles above the present city of Inchelium (ZIP 99138).

Nchumutastum, home of the Snchumutast (about 6 miles above Nilamin).

Nilamin, home of the Snilaminak (about 15 miles above kakalapia).

Nkuasiam, home of the Snkuasik (slightly above the present town of Daisy [ZIP 99120] the opposite side of the river).

Smichunulau, home of the Smichunulauk (at the site of the present bridge over Columbia River, Highway 395, at Kettle Falls).

History: The history of the Colville was similar to that of the neighboring tribes except that Kettle Falls was early fixed upon as the site of an important post by the Hudson Bay Company and brought with it the usual advantages and disadvantages of white contact.

Population:

```
1780   1,000 (Mooney, 1928)
1805   2,500 (Lewis and Clark)
1904     321 (Swanton)
1907     334 (Swanton)
1937     322 (Swanton)
1987   (See Appendix)
```

Names by which remembered: A reservation, city (ZIP 99114); early Fort Colville.

Copalis

Also called:

Che-pa-lis, meaning "opposite the rock."

Linguistic group: Salishan, coastal division

Location: Along the Copalis River and at its mouth, as well as along the ocean frontage between Joe Creek and Grays Harbor, opposite Copalis Rock, the rock about two miles offshore to the north of the city.

Population:

```
1805   200 (Lewis and Clark)
1888     5 (Olsen)
```

History: Lewis and Clark reported this tribe occupied 10 houses. The tribe is presumed to have been moved to a reservation, but data is elusive.

Names by which remembered: A river; city (post office 1890-1905); city Copalis Beach (ZIP 98535); Copalis Crossing (ZIP 98536); -head (navigation); -rock (navigation).

Cowlitz
Cow-e-lis-kee (Cow-e-lis-ke)
Also called:

> Nu-so-lupsh, name used by Indians not on Puget Sound applied to Upper Cowlitz and to Upper Chehalis.
> Ta-wa-l-litch, "capturing the medicine spirit."

Linguistic group: Salishan, coastal division
Location: Along both the lower and middle course of Cowlitz (earlier: Coweliskee) River.
Villages:

> Ray (1932) gives: Awi'mani, at the mouth of Coweman River, south of Kelso, and Manse'la, on site of Longview. (See Curtis, 1907-9.)

Population:

1780	1,000 (Mooney, 1928; includes Chehalis, Humptulips and others)
1853	165 (Gibbs, includes Upper Chehalis)
1887	127 (Puyallup Reservation)
1910	105 (U.S. Census)
1923	490 (U.S. Indian Office, may include others)
1987	(See Appendix)

Names by which remembered: A river, mountain pass; glacier; county; park; chimneys (high rock towers); cleaver (rocky ridge); bay; box canyon; divide (in mountains); landing (on Cowlitz River—now Toledo, ZIP 98591); trail; town (post office 1854-1880, 1881-1906).

Duwamish

Location and villages:

A. The Duwamish River from its mouth up to and including the Black and Cedar Rivers, with the following villages:
Dsidsila'letc, at Yesler Way and Jackson St., Seattle.
Duwe'kwulsh, at Maple Valley.
Kati'lbabsh, at the present City of Renton (ZIP 98055).
Sakwe'kwewad, on Cedar River about two miles from Renton.
Skwa'lko, where the Black and White Rivers join to form the Duwamish.
Tkwabko', at the south end of Lake Washington (Renton).
Tola'ltu, below Duwamish Head, Seattle.
Tupa'thlteb, at the mouth of the easternmost estuary of the Duwamish.
Tuduwa'bsh, at the mouth of the Duwamish River.

B. From where the Black River flows into the Duwamish to the junction of the White and Green Rivers, including these villages:
Stak and Tcutupa'lhu, on the east bank of the White River between its junction with the Black River and the mouth of the Green River.

C. The Green River villages:
Ila'lkoabsh, at the junction of the Green and White Rivers.
Su'sabsh, on Suise Creek.
Perhaps several groups of houses: (1) on the upper Green River, including Tskoka'bid (at the bend now spanned by the highway bridge about four miles east of Auburn, ZIP 98002); (2) on the north bank on former Wooding Ranch; (3) on former Du Bois Ranch; (4) at the mouth of Newaukum Creek.

D. The White River village, Sbalko'absh (on White River near a small stream at the southeast corner of Muckleshoot Reservation and to the east on Boise Creek).

E. The Lake Washington people, including the Thluwi'thalbsh (at Union Bay), the Sammamish (at the mouth of Sammamish River), and the peoples of Salmon Bay. In 1856 they were removed to the eastern shore of Bainbridge Island. As the place lacked a fishing ground they were afterward taken to Holderness Point, on the west side of Eliot Bay, which was already a favorite fishing place. Assigned to Tulalip Reservation in recent years.

Linguistic group: Salishan, Nisqually dialect
History: Noted for spirit canoe ceremony. Shamans

staged this event in winter to recapture departed souls of those that might have become lost while on the way to the spirit world. The program includes special dances, music as well as the medicine man's magic. The ceremony was a "pay" event, the costs handled by the family of the person whose soul was presumed lost.

Population:

```
1780   1,200 (Mooney, 1928)
1856      64 (one reporter claimed 312, which
              seems high)
1910      20 (U.S. Census)
1987   (See Appendix)
```

Names by which remembered: Tribe was located on site of present city of Seattle, the city's name from a Duwamish chief, Chief Sealth; a river; bay (now Elliott Bay); head (navigation); town (post office 1860-1864, 1874-1901—now Georgetown ZIP 98108).

Hoh

Also called:

Oh-la-qu-hoh
Hooh-oh-ah-lat, "can speak Quinault at that place."

Linguistic group: Chimakuan, remotely associated with Salishan. The Hoh spoke the Quileute language and was often considered a part of that tribe.

Location: Along the Hoh River.

History: A reservation was established for the Hoh by Presidential Executive Order on September 11, 1893. The site was 40 miles south of Cape Flattery and was of 443 acres.

Population:

```
1780   500 (Mooney, 1928; Hoh and
            Quileute)
1905    62 (Hoh only)
```

Names by which remembered: Town (post office 1904-1934); creek; head (navigation); reservation; lake; river.

Humptulips
Ho-to-la-bixh, "hard to polle" (chilly region).
Linguistic group: Salishan, coastal division. Closely related to Chehalis.
Location: Along the Humptulips River, Hoquiam River, Wishkah River, on both north and south shores of Grays Harbor.
Villages:

> Hli'mumi (Curtis, 1907-9), near North Cove (see Note about cove under Chinook).
> Hoquiam, on Hoquiam River.
> Hooshkal (Gibbs), on the north shore of Grays Harbor.
> Kishkallen (Gibbs), on the north shore of Grays Harbor.
> Klimmim (Gibbs, 1877).
> Kplelch (Curtis), at the mouth of North River (Willapa Bay).
> Kwapks (Curtis, 1907-9), at the mouth of North River.
> Mo'nilumsh (Curtis), at Georgetown.
> Nooachhummik (Gibbs), on the coast north of Grays Harbor.
> Nookalthu (Gibbs), north of Grays Harbor.
> Nu'moihanhl (Curtis), at Tokeland (ZIP 98590).
> Whishkah, (post office 1882-two months; 1904-1917, 1978-two months), on Wishkah River.

Population:

> 1888   18 (Olsen)
> 1904   21 (Olsen)

Names by which remembered: River; city (ZIP 98552).

Kalispel (See Idaho)

Klickitat
Also called:

> Cladachut, by Chinooks ("Indians beyond the mountains").
> Klackatat
> Awi-adshi, Molalla name. Lûk'-a-tatt, Puyallup name.

Máhane, Umpqua name. Milauq'-tcu-wûn'-ti, Alsea name, meaning "scalpers."

Mûn-an'-ne-qu' tûnne, Naltunnetunne name, meaning "inland people" Qwûlh-hwai-pûm, own name, meaning "prairie people."

Tlakäi'tat, Okanagon name.

Tse la'kayat amim, Kalapuya name.

T¡uwanxa-ikc, Clatsop name.

Wahnookt, Cowlitz name.

Linguistic group: Shapwailutan, Shahaptian division. Subdivisions and villages:

Possibly the Atanum or Atanumlema should be added to the Klickitat. Mooney (1928) reports that their language was distinct, though related to, both Klickitat and Yakima.

Itkilak or Ithlkilak, at White Salmon Landing, which they occupied jointly with the Chilluckquittequaw.

Nanshuit (occupied jointly with the Chilluckquittequaw), at Underwood (ZIP 98651).

Shgwaliksh, not far below Memaloose Island.

Tgasgutcu (occupied jointly with the Chilluckquittequaw), said to be about ½ mile west of a long high mountain opposite Mosier, Ore. (ZIP 97040), and about one mile above White Salmon Landing, but the exact location remains in question.

Wiltkun (exact location unknown.)

History: The original home of the Klickitat was somewhere south of the Columbia and they invaded their later territory after the Yakima crossed the river. IN 1805 Lewis and Clark found them wintering on Yakima and Klickitat Rivers.

The Klickitats were very active traders and profited by becoming "middle-men" between the coast tribes and the inland tribes as it was across Klickitat territory that goods-in-trade had to pass.

Swanton says that due to fever epidemic in the Willamette Valley, the Klickitat ventured there on trading missions. Neils claims these were horse stealing ventures. Nicandri, in his *Northwest Chiefs* points out several chiefs got together and went on missions all the way to Sutter's Fort, near Sacramento, to trade furs and horses for cattle. On this trip Chief Peu-peu-mox-mox's son, who had the

Christian name Elijah Hedding, was murdered in cold blood by an American brigand. The chief, from then on, was only a "faint friend" of the whites. Apparently, partially in revenge, the Chief sent 20 Klickitats with 30 Yakimas to the cascades of the Columbia for a raid on the settlements there, including at The Dalles, with the purpose of killing all the whites in the area. On the 26th of March, 1856, the Indians attacked surprising the settlers who ran for cover but some were killed. The Indians burned the dock, houses, warehouse and sawmill. Nearly all of the army troops were elsewhere but on word of the attack, headed back to The Dalles. In the meantime, Lt. Philip H. Sheridan, with a detachment of dragoons and a small ship's salute cannon, took passage upstream for the relief of the settlers. Although the Yakimas had sent large reinforcements, the "Cascades Massacre" was over in a few days. Lt. Sheridan wrote that his detachment captured thirteen "of the principal miscreants," established their guilt and turned these Indians over to Colonel George Wright for trial. Nine were hung.

This tribe joined in the treaty of June 9, 1855, thus ceding their land to the federal government. Most of them were settled on the Yakima Reservation.

Population:

    1780   600 (including Taitinapam, Mooney, 1928)
    1805   700 (Lewis and Clark)
    1910   405 (U.S. Census)

Names by which remembered: Known as great traders, the "wheelers and dealers" of their day and location. A river; county; creek in Lewis County; a creek in Mt. Rainier National Park; glacier; landing—now Lyle (ZIP 98635); prairie; city (ZIP 98628).

Kwaiailk
    Also called:

    Kluck-ulium, by Wilkes.

Kwu-teh-ni, Kwalhioqua name.
Nu-so-lupsh, by Sound Indians, referring to the rapids of their stream.
Stak-ta-mish, a name for this and other inland tribes, meaning "forest people."
Upper Chehalis, common name.

Linguistic group: Salishan, coastal division.
Location: Upper Chehalis River.
History and village: Cloquallum, on Cloquallum River. The Wilkes Expedition borrowed the word Klu-kwe-li-ub, the Chehalis' word for the Quillayute Indians, and found the first three syllables referred to a ceremonial dance of a secret society. The dance was alleged to gain magic powers during wars. The final syllable's translation could very well be "we are the people of a very dangerous Being thus you [enemy] should be afraid of us [because we are charge with magic]. Wilkes visited the area in 1841.
Population:

1855   216 (Gibbs)

About this time the tribe became intertwined with the Cowlitz.

Kwalhioqua
From a Chinook designation means, "from a lonely place in the forest."
Also called:

Axwe'lapc, "people of the Willapa," by the Chinook and Quinault Indians.
Gila'q!ulawas, from the name of the place where they usually lived.
Owhillapsh or Willapa, applied to this tribe erroneously.
Tkulhiyogoa'ick, Chinook name.

Linguistic group: Athapascan.
Location: Upper end of Willapa River and the southern and western headwaters of the Chehalis River. Gibbs (1877) concluded that the tribe lived in an extended area east of the

Cascade Mountains, however Boas (1892) fails to agree.
Subdivisions: ??
Population:

1780   200 (Mooney, 1928)
1846   100 (Hale)
1850   2 males, "several females." (If this count is accepted,
       then the 1846 enumeration would be in error unless an
       unrecorded fatal disease hit the tribe.)

Reasons why remembered: Although a member of the
Athapascan group, was the only tribe in that group in
Washington in historic times.

Lummi

Also spelled há-lum-mi, or Nuh-lum-mi, or Qtlumi.
Also called:

Nukhlésh, by the Skagit, who also included the Clallam in the
   designation.
N'wh-ah-tk-hm, the tribal name, also for Whatcom Falls.

Linguistic group: Salishan, coastal division. Believed to
have spoken same dialect as Songish Indians of Vancouver
Island, Canada.
Location: Along the northern shore of Bellingham Bay
and at the confluence with the Nooksack River. Some bands
in the San Juan Islands which are marked (*) in the list of
villages. Following a treaty, the tribe was placed on the
Lummi Reservation.
Villages:

Elek, near the north end of Bellingham Bay.
Hwetlkiem, near the north end of Bellingham Bay west of
   Nooksack River.
Kwakas, on the north side of Nooksack River.
Momli, near the mouth of Nooksack River. Skalisan, north of
   Point Francis and opposite Lummi Island.
Fishing villages:
Hoholos, a point on Orcas Island south of Freeman Island*.
Hwitcosang, in Upright Channel south of Shaw Island*.

Hwtcihom or Bee Station, north of Sandy Point (on reservation).
Skalekushan or Village Point, on Lummi Island.
Skoletc, on Lopez Island opposite town of Lopez (ZIP 98261)*.
Tceltenem, Point Roberts (ZIP 98281).
Tikwoloks, on Orcas Island*.

Population:

1780	1,000 (includes Nooksack and Samish—Mooney, 1928)
1905	412 (Swanton)
1910	353 (B.I.A.)
1923	505 (B.I.A.)
1937	661 (B.I.A.)
1978	(See Appendix)

Names by which remembered: Town (post office 1874-1894); town Lummi Island (ZIP 98262); bay; reservation; island; peak; river; rocks (navigation).

Makah
Meaning: "people-who-live-on-point-projecting-into-the-sea" but commonly just called "cape people."
Also called:

Klasset
Micaw
Makaw
Ba-qa-o, Puyallup name
Cape Flattery Indians, from their location.
Classet, Nootka name, meaning "outsiders."
Kwe-net-che-chat, own name, meaning "cape people."
Tla'asath, Nootka name, meaning "outside people."

Linguistic group: Wakashan, Nootka branch.
Location: On Cape Flattery and along the south coast of Strait of Juan de Fuca to the Hoko River, then south on the sea front to Flattery Rocks, also on Tatoosh Island. Their own land was classed as reservation, thus this tribe was not moved.
Villages:

Winter towns:

Baada, on Neah Bay.

Neah, on the site of old Spanish fort, Port Nuñez Gaona, Neah Bay.

Ar-kut-tle-kower, at mouth of Waatch River on coast 3½ miles south of Cape Flattery.

Summer villages:

Ahchawat, at Cape Flattery. Kehsidatsoos, location unknown.

Kiddekubbut, 3 miles from Neah Bay.

Tatooche, on Tatoosh Island, off Cape Flattery.

History: The Maka released their tribal land to the U.S. Government by treaty of 1855 but were not consolidated for reservation living until 1893. Although the tribe lost a good portion of its original claim, for the most part none of its members had to move as the new reservation was on the northwest corner of their land. After World War II the tribal council purchased a surplus U.S. Army warehouse and camp area on Neah Bay which became their reservation headquarters.

Population:

1780	2,000 (combined with Ozette—Mooney, 1928)
1905	435 (Swanton)
1910	360 (U.S. Census)
1923	425 (includes Ozette—B.I.A.)
1937	407 (Makah only—B.I.A.)
1985	919 (Yenne)
1987	(See Appendix)

Names by which remembered: Makah and Ozette are the only tribes of Wakashan group, Nootka branch in the U.S. reservation.

Methow

Also called:

Smee-the-owe, "sun."

Buttle-mule-emauch, the name of the river on which they resided.

Linguistic group: Salishan.

Location: On Methow (Buttle-mule-emauch) River. A band, the Chilowhist, spent winters along the Okanogan River between Sand Point and Malott (ZIP 98829).
Population:

1780 800 (combined with Columbia—Mooney, 1928)
1907 324 (Swanton)

Names by which remembered: City (98834); river; valley.

Mical
Linguistic group: Shahaptian, (Pshwanwapam).
Location: Along upper Nisqually River.
Population: Not enumerated separately.

Muckleshoot
Also called:

Skopamish.

Linguistic group: Salishan, Nisqually dialect.
Location: Along the White River extending from about Kent (ZIP 98031) east toward the mountains, as well as along the Green River.
Subdivisions: The following names appear applied to bands in their territory:

Sekamish, on White River.
Skopamish, on upper Green River.
Smulkamish, on upper White River.
Smith (1940) adds Dothliuk, at South Prairie below where Cole Creek enters South Prairie Creek, a branch of Carbon River.

Population:

1780 1,200 (includes Nisqually, Puyallup—Mooney, 1928)
1863 222 (apparently Skopamish only—Swanton)
1870 183 (apparently Smulkamish only—Swanton)
1907 780 (Mooney, 1928)

1937   194 (all branches—B.I.A.)
1970   2,370 (Muckleshoot Reservation)
1987   (See Appendix)

Names by which remembered: A reservation, prairie.

Neketemeuk

Presumed to have been a Salishan linguistic tribe at an unknown early period in vicinity above The Dalles, plausibly on both the Washington and/or Oregon side of the Columbia River. There seems no definitive study to firmly establish such a tribe existed.

Nespelem (See Sanpoil)

Nez Perce (See Idaho)

Nisqually

Also called:

> Nasqually
> Nezqually
> Niskwalli
> N'skwali
> Sig-gwal-it-chie
> Skwale'absh (Quallyamish, Skwalliamhmish)—name of the river.
> Askwalli, Calapooya name
> Lts χe'als, Nestucca name.
> Suketi'kenuk, Sukoti'kenuk, by Columbia Indians along with all other coast people, meaning "people of the other side," with reference to the Cascade Mountains.
> Tse Skua'lli ami'm, Luckamiute Kalapooian name.

Linguistic group: Salishan, coastal division.

Location: Along Nisqually River above its mouth and on the middle and upper route of Puyallup River.

Subdivisions and villages:

> Basha'labsh, on Mashel River and neighboring Nisqually river, the town on a highland below Eatonville (ZIP 98328) on Mashel River.

Sakwi'absh, Clear Creek and neighboring Nisqually River, the main settlement on a hill near confluence of Clear Creek and Nisqually River.

Sigwa'letcabsh, on Segualitcu River, the main settlement where Dupont Creek enters the Sqwualitcu River. (Neither of these creeks are mentioned by Hitchman.)

Tsakwe'kwabsh, on Clarks Creek and neighboring Puyallup River, the main settlement where Clarks Creek empties into Puyallup river, but seems to have included also Skwa'dabsh, at the mouth of a creek entering Wapato Creek above the Wapato Creek village.

Sta'habsh, where the Stuck River enters the Puyallup.

Tsuwa'diabsh, on what is now th Puyallup River above its junction with the Carbon River at Orting (ZIP 98360) just below the site of the Soldiers' Home.

Tuwha'khabsh, east of Orting, where Vogt Creek enters the Carbon River.

Yisha'ktcabsh, on Nisqually Lake, the principal settlement being at the mouth of a large creek.

Yokwa'lsshabsh, on Muck Creek and the neighboring parts of Nisqually River, the main settlement located where Muck Creek enters Nisqually River, and a division on Clover Creek.

Population:

1780	3,600 (Mooney, 1928)
1907	1,150 (approx.—Swanton)
1910	1,100 (approx.—U.S. Census)
1937	62 (B.I.A.)
1985	1,726 (Yenne)
1987	(See Appendix)

Names by which remembered: Town (post office 1860-1865, 1915-1960, 1961-1966); name of heavily-traveled entrance to Mt. Rainier National Park; flats; glacier; head (navigation); Fort Nisqually; Nisqually House; reservation; lake; reach (navigation); reservoir; river.

Nooksack
Also called:

Neuk-sack (Nootsaak), "fern-eating people," also Nooksak, Nooksach.

Linguistic group: Salishan, coastal division. At one time it is presumed the Nooksack separated from Squawmish of British Columbia and spoke the same language.
Location: On Nooksack River.
Population:

1906 200 (Swanton)
1910   85 (U.S. Census)
1937 239 (B.I.A.)
1985 860 (Nooksack Reservation)
1987 (See Appendix)

Names by which remembered: Town (ZIP 98276); Nooksack Community; falls; river.

Ntlakyapamuk
Hunting trips into Washington from Canada. No known villages or bands lived in Washington. (See Canada)

Okanagon
Also called:

Akênuq'la'lam or KokEnu'k'ke, by Kutenai (Chamberlain, 1892).
Isonkuaíli, own name, meaning "our people."
Kank.'utla'atlam, Kutenai name, meaning "flatheads" (Boas, 1911).
KEnake'n, by Tobacco Plains Band of Klickitat.
Okanigen.
Koinakane.
Okanagen.
O-kan-Okan.
OtcEnake', Otcæna.qai'n, or Utcæna'.qai'n, by the Salish and their allies.
Soo-wan'-a-mooh, Shuswap name.
.SoqEnäqai'mEx, Columbia name.
Tcutzwa'ut, Tcitxûa'ut, Tsawa'nEmux, or OkEna.qai'n, Ntlakyapamuk names.
WEtc.naqei'n, Skitswish name.

Linguistic group: Salishan, interior division with closest relatives being Colville, Sanpoil, Senijextee.
Locations and villages: Along the Okanogan River

above the confluence with Similkameen River, British Columbia, in vicinity of Hedley and Princeton as well as in Washington. For the purpose of attempting not to dismember the classifications of the Okanogan Tribe, the editor shows both the Canadian and Washington portions. The Similkameen Okanagon were divided into three bands, the Okanagon proper into four; with the villages belonging to each they are as follows:

Upper Similkameen Band:
  Ntkaihelok (Ntkai'xelôx), about 11 miles below Princeton, north side of Similkameen River.
  Snazaist (Snäzäi'st), on the north shore of Similkameen River, a little east of Twenty-mile Creek and the town of Hedley.
  Tcutcuwiha (Tcutcuwîxa) or Tcutcawiha (Tcutcawi'xa), on the north side of Similkameen River, a little below the preceding.
Ashnola Band:
  Ashnola (Acnu'lôx), on the south side of Similkameen River, near the mouth of Ashnola Creek.
  Nsrepus (Nsre'pus) or Skanek, .sa'nɛx, a little below the Ashnola, but on the north side of Similkameen River.
Lower Similkameen Band:
  Kekerɛmyeaus (Kekerɛmye'aus), across Similkameen River from Keremyeus.
  Keremyeus (Kerɛmye'us), on the north side of Similkameen river, near Keremeos.
  Nkura-elok (Nkurae'lôx), on the south side of Similkameen River and about four miles below Kerɛmyeaus.
  Ntleuktan (Ntleuxta'n), on the south side of Similkameen River, opposite Skemkain.
  Skemkain (Skemquai'n), a short distance below Nkuraelok.
  Smelalok (Smela'lox), on the south side of Similkameen River, about 10 miles below Nsrepus.

To the villages listed above must be added the following old Similkameen village sites in Washington:

  Hepulok (Xe'pulôx).
  Konkonetp (Ko'nkonetp), near the mouth of Similkameen river.
  Kwahalos (Kwaxalo's), a little back from Similkameen River, below Hepulok.
  Naslitok (Na.sli'tok), just across the International Boundary in Washington.

Skwa'nnt, below Kwahalos.

Tsakeiskenemuk (Tsakei'sxɛnɛmux), on a creek along the trail between Keremeous and Penticton.

Tseltsalo's, below Kwahalos.

Douglas Lake Band:

Kathlemik (Ka.'lɛmix), near Guichons, at the mouth of the Upper Nicola river, where it falls into Nicola Lake.

Komkonatko (Komkona'tko) or Komkenatk (Komkɛna'tkk), at Fish Lake on the headwaters of the Upper Nicola River.

Kwiltcana (Kwiltca'na) at the mouth of Quilchene Creek.

Spahamen (Spa'xamɛn) or Spahamen (Späxɛmɛn), at Douglas Lake.

Komaplix or Head of the Lake Band:

Nkamapeleks (Nkama'pɛlɛks) or Nkomapeleks (Nkoma'pɛlɛks), near the head of Okanagan Lake, aobut eight miles north of Vernon.

Nkekemapeleks (Nkekema'pɛlɛks), at the head of Long Lake, a little over a mile from Vernon.

Nkokosten (Nxok.o'stɛn), a place near Kelowna, and also a general name for the district around there and Mission.

Skelaunna (Skɛla'un.na), at Kelowna, near the present town.

Sntlemukten (Sntlɛmuxte'n), (Black Town), a little north of the head of Okanagan Lake.

Stekatelkeneut (Stekatelxene'ut), a little above Mission(?) on Long Lake opposite Tselotsus.

Tseketku (Tse'kɛtku), at a small lake a little north of Black Town.

Tselotsus (Tsɛlo'tsus), at the narrows of Long Lake.

Tskelhokem (Tsxɛlho'qɛm), near the lower end of Long Lake about 19 miles south of Vernon.

Penticton Band:

Penticton (Penti'ktɛn), Penticton, near the foot of Okanagan Lake.

Stekatkothlkneut (Stɛkatkolxne'ut) or Stekatethlkeneut (Stɛ katɛlxɛe'ut), on the opposite side of Long Lake from Mission.

Nkamip Band:

Nkamip (Nkami'p), on the east side of the upper end of Osoyoos Lake.

Sci'yus, near Haynes or the old customhouse just north of the American line.

Skohenetk (Sxoxene'tkuᵘ), at the lower end of Dog Lake.

To the villages listed above must be added the following names of old village sites on Okanagan River in Washington:

Milkemahituk (Milkɛmaxi-tuk) or Miklemihituk (Milkɛ-mixi'tuk), a general name for the district around the mouth of Similkameen River and of the river itself.

Okinaken Okina'qen), an old name for Sathlilk.

Sathlilk (Sali'lx), near the mouth of Similkameen River.

Smɛlkammin (Smelkammi'n), thought to be the old name of a place at the mouth of Similkameen River.

History: The Okanagon differed little from that of the Ntlakyapamuk and other neighboring tribes except that they were affecting by having parts of the tribe on both sides of the American and Canadian border. During the last 250 years, however, there has been a steady displacement from the U.S.

Population (according to Swanton, includes Sinkaietk):

1780	2,200 (Mooney, 1928)
	2,500-3,000 (Teit, 1900)
1905	1,516 (Canada: 824; U.S.: 692)
1906	1,351 (Canada: no change; U.S.: 527)
1967	1,503 (U.S.—Yenne)
1987	(See Appendix)

Names by which remembered: County, city (ZIP 98840); ghost town (post office 1884-1888); National Forest; river, all in Washington.

Ozette
Also called:

O-se-ilth
O-se-elth ("middle tribe")

Linguistic group: Wakashan. Nootka branch of Makah
Location: Along the Ozette River and lake.
Villages:

Ozette, at Flattery Rocks
Sooes, four miles south of the Makah village at Waatch
Tsooess (Tsooyes)

History: This small tribe operated from two so-called permanent villages until the members were provided a

153

reservation in their own region now at the northern tip of Olympia National Park. The reservation was activated in 1893. Hitchman wrote that the last Ozette Indian died in 1953 and the reservation is abandoned.

Population:

 1780 2,000 (combined with Makah; Mooney, 1928)
 1937 1 (Swanton)
 1953 1 (Hitchman)

Names by which remembered: Village (post office 1891-1900, 1902-1914, 1927-1942); reservation; island; lake; U.S. Coast Guard Beach Patrol Station guarding against plausible Japanese invasion during WW-II as detailed by Webber in *SILENT SIEGE-II: Japanese Attacks On North America in World War II.*

Palouse
Also called:

Palloatpallah, by Lewis and Clark.
Spalu'.sox, said to be a place name.

Linguistic group: Shapwailian. Shahaptian division. Closely associated with Nez Perce. (See Idaho)
Location: Along the Palouse river in Idaho and Washington as well as along a small section of Snake River. Seasonal villages in the camas grounds near Moscow.
Subdivisions and villages:

Almotu (Almota) on north bank Snake River.
Chimnapum, on the northwest side of Columbia River near the mouth of Snake River and on Lower Yakima River.
Kasispa, at Ainsworth, at the junction of Snake and Columbia Rivers.
Palus, on the north bank of Snake river just below its junction with the Palouse.
Sokulk or Wanapum, on Columbia River above the mouth of Snake River.
Tasawiks, on the north bank of Snake river, about 15 miles above its mouth.

154

History: Palouse tribe believed to have been related to Yakima. The tribe has been described as outcasts, outlaws and renegades by Trafzer and Scheuerman, who assert the Palouse had a hand in the Whitman Massacre (See Cayuse) and because the tribe was, of a body, against white encroachment on their land. Refused to sign 1855 treaty thus no reservation was created for them. Faced with nowhere to go and being pushed constantly by settlers on their own land the Palouse became outcasts.
Population:

1780	5,400 (Mooney, 1928)
1805	1,600 (Lewis and Clark)
1854	500 (Swanton)
1910	82 (U.S. Census)

Names by which remembered: City (ZIP 99161); "Palouse City"—historical—at confluence of Snake and Palouse Rivers; state park; -hills (wheat farming primarily in Whitman County) railroad junction (now Connell); river.

Pshwanwapam
Also called:

Upper Yakima.

Name means "on the stony ground."
Linguistic group: Shapwailutan. Shahaptian division.
Location: On upper areas of Yakima River.

Puyallup
Pwiya'lap, Indian name for river.
Linguistic group: Salishan. Nisqually dialect of the coastal division.
Location: At mouth of Puyallup (pron: pew-ahl-upp) River and coastal area of Puget Sound, with some activity on Vashon Island as well as at Carr Inlet.
Subdivisions and villages:

Esha'ktlabsh, on Hylebos Waterway.

Kalka'lak, at the mouth of Wapato Creek.

Klbalt, at Glencove.

Puyallup or Spwiya'laphabsh, on Commencement Bay and Puyallup River as far up as the mouth of Clarks Creek, including the main settlement at mouth of Puyallup River.

Sha'tckad, where Clay Creek empties into Puyallup River.

Sko'tlbabsh, on Carr Inlet, including a Sko'tlbabsh settlement on Carr Inlet above the town of Minter.

Skwapa'bsh, on the south part of Vashon Island and west of the Narrows, including a town, same name, at mouth of a stream at Gig Harbor (ZIP 98335).

Skwlo'tsid, at head of Wollochet Bay.

Steilacoom, on Steilacoom Creek and neighboring beach, the main village on present site of Steilacoom (ZIP 98388).

Tsugwa'lethl, at Quartermaster Harbor.

Tule'lakle, at the head of Burley Lagoon, Carr Inlet.

Twa'debshab, at the mouth of a creek formerly entering Commencement Bay and now covered by Tacoma (ZIP 98400).

History: Tribe name stands for "generous people." The Puyallup participated in the treaty of Medicine Creek in 1854 and were allowed a 33-acre reservation. As this was determined to be insufficient, a Presidential Executive Order in 1873 enlarged it to eventually cover 17,645 acres. The Cushman General Hospital, set up to handle all medical requirements of Indians in the state, was located here. In recent years the hospital has seen improvement with the times and is now operated as the Health Authority of the Puyallup Tribe of Indians. In addition to being a general medical and surgical facility, there are special units that deal with alcohol and drug tratment, children's services and a full dental clinic. A regular outreach program is conducted and there is the Kwawachee Mental Health Center. There is a nutrition department as well as full pharmacy.

The Puyallup Tribe of Indians also operates Chief Leschi Elementary School as well as Chief Leschi High School.

The reservation is on the north edge of downtown Tacoma at the Interstate 5 and Puyallup off ramp. The beautiful grounds can be seen from the freeway.

Population:

    1937   322 (B.I.A.)
    1985   7,158 (Puyallup Reservation)
    1987   (See Appendix)

Names by which remembered: City (ZIP 98371); cleaver—Mt. Rainier National Park; glacier; reservation; river.

Queets (Quaitso)
Linguistic group: Salishan, coastal division. Closely related to Quinault.
Location: Along Queets River and tributaries.
History: Name is from a legend meaning "out from the dirt comes the skin." When the Great Spirit waded in the river and on rubbing his legs for circulation on walking onto the land, he tossed the dirt which came off his legs into the river then out came a man and a woman thus forming Quaitso tribe from which the meaning is taken.
Population:

    1780   1,500 (with Quinault—Mooney, 1928)
    1805   250 (Lewis and Clark reported the tribe in 18 houses.)
    1909   62 (Swanton)
    1936   82 (Olsen, 1936)

Names by which remembered: Town (post office 1892-1905, 1916, 1921); corridor in Olympia National Park; glacier; river.

Quileute (Quillayute)
Also spelled:

Quillehute   Quallayute
Quillyhuyte   Quelaiault
Keilleute

Linguistic group: Chimakuan. Remotely related to

Wakashan and Salishan.

Location: Along the Quillayute River.

History: A reservation was finally set aside in 1889 following the treaty of 1855 for this tribe. The area was 595 acres and was at the mouth of the Quillayute River at today's city of LaPush (ZIP 98350). In some publications the government spells the name "Quileute" but this spelling seems unique to an earlier error. Note that the name of the river does not appear on most maps as the river is but five miles long, taking that name at the confluence of the Bogachiel and Soleduck Rivers east of LaPush.

Population:

1780	500 (includes Hoh)
1888	64 (Olson, 1936; probably low or Quileute only—?)
1910	303 (U.S. Census)
1937	284 (B.I.A.)
1970	270 (Yenne)
1985	383 (Yenne)
1987	(See Appendix)

Names and reasons why remembered: Uniqueness of language, spoken only by Quileute, Hoh and Chimakum. Needle (navigation); prairie; river; ghost town (post office 1879-1914, 1927-1937).

Quinault

Also called:

Kwle-ni-lth
Wi-n-nilth.

Linguistic group: Chimakuan. Possibly related to Wakashan along with the Chimakum and Hoh.

Location: Along the Quinault River and lake as well as along the coast between Raft River and Joe Creek. Largest present "village" is town of Taholah (ZIP 98587).

Subdivisions: As associate band (tribe?) or division was mentioned by Lewis and Clark.

Villages:

A'alatsis, three miles below Lake Quinault.

Djagaka'lmik, ½ mile above Nosklako's.

Djekwe'ls, on the north bank of Quinault River about 400 yards above Thlathle'-lap.

Gutse'lps, six miles below Lake Quinault.

Hagwi'shtap, about 1½ miles above Cook Creek.

He'shnithl or Kuku'mnithl, on the south bank of Quinault River about 500 yards above Pini'lks.

Kwakwa'h, not far from Hagwi'shtap.

Kwakwa'nikatctan, four miles below Lake Quinault.

Kwatai'tamik, three miles above Kwakwa'h.

Kwatai'tumik, on the south bank about 500 yards above Kwi'naithl.

Kwikwa'la, perhaps ½ mile above Sunuksunu'ham.

Kwi'naithl, at present site of Taholah (ZIP 98587).

Lae'lsnithl, on north bank a mile or less above Heshnithl.

La'lshithl, perhaps a mile above Djagaka'lmik on Quinault River.

Ma'atnithl, one mile below the fork of upper Quinault River.
(There are two forks on the river above the lake.—Ed.)

Magwa'ksnithl, 300 yards above Kwikwa'la.

Me'tsugutsathlan, on south bank of Quinault River at its mouth.

Nago'olatcan, not far from Nossho'k.

Negwe'thlan, at the mouth of Cook Creek.

Nokedja'kt or Thla'a'lgwap, on south bank a few hundrd yards above Tonans.

Nomi'lthlostan, just above Kwakwa'h.

No'omo'thlaspsh, at mouth of Moclips River at Moclips (ZIP 98562).

No'omo'thlapshtcu, not far above Magwa'ksnithl.

No'skathlan, a few miles above Kwi'naithl, on the north bank of Quinault River.

Noskthlako's, on south bank of Quinault River perhaps one mile above No'skathlan.

Nossho'k, not far above Nokedja'kt.

No'sthluk, not far from Djekwe'ls.

Pina'alathl, located where the upper Quinault River enters Lake Quinault.

Pini'lks, close to La'lshithl.

Pino'otcan tci'ta, on the upper Quinault below Ma'anithl.

Po'iks, on the upper Quinault above Finley Creek.

Pote'lks, one mile above Tsimi'sh.

Sunuksunu'ham, not far from Nomi'lthlostan.

Tamo'ulgutan, just below No'omo'thlapshtcu.

Tci'tano'sklakalathl, at the outlet of Lake Quinault. (Amanda Park, ZIP 98526.)

Thlathle'lap, at the mouth of Quinault River on the north
bank between river and Cape Elizabeth.
To'nans, less than ½ mile above He'shnithl.
Tsi'i'sh, two miles above Magwaksnithl.

History: The first encounter with the Quinaults appears
to have been in 1775 with the landing of the Spaniards at
about where the city of Moclips is today. The spanish decided
to establish a mission here, among the Indians, based on their
claim that all lands along the Pacific Ocean belonged to
them by right of discovery with subsequent exploration.
This "right" had been proclaimed by Balboa in 1513, in
which year he discovered the Pacific Ocean, and had been
carried out by his followers in several voyages of discovery
as late as 1779. Literature available to the editor is unclear
whether the encounter between the Quinaults and the
Spanish was victorious for which side, Yenne claiming that
after "the first bloody encounter," the Spanish set up their
mission. One may presume the Quinaults lost. While a
specific date of Spanish withdrawal is elusive, if indeed such
is actually known, the Adams-Onis Treaty of 1819 terminated all Spanish influence north of the present Oregon-
California line (42° N.). Accordingly, the Spanish mission
closed and the occupants left.

On July 1, 1885, the Quinaults signed a treaty with the
U.S. Government which paved the way for the establishment of the boundaries of the Quinault Reservation. The
plan was to contain all the western Washington coastal
Indians here, but due to inability of the various tribes to get
out of the plan what each wanted, several reservations were
created from Cape Flattery to Moclips.

With an area full of old-growth timber, large-scale
commercial logging began on the reservation in 1922.
During the next twenty years there were large forest fires in
the area because there had been no forest management plan,
which today includes replanting in the cut over areas, as
tons of waste—"slash"—had been left behind. By the mid-
1970s, the tribe, with the assistance of university-level study
groups, private industry and the government, had developed

a comprehensive program for the Quinault timber interests.

The once pristine coastline along the reservation's frontage was being inundated with "litter" and frequent fires in driftwood were causing grave concerns. Thus, in the late 1960s, the tribe closed its 25-mile long beach to all non-Indians. Large billboard-size signs were posted on the highways at the reservation's boundaries warning non-Indians that tribal laws were being enforced. A Beach Lands Ordinance ("Title 52" March 28, 1970) cites Presidential Executive Order of November 14, 1873, referring to the treaty of July 1, 1855 (12 Stat. 971) "land including beach lands along the Pacific Ocean above the 'low water mark . . . no person shall deface or destroy natural beauty, objects of nature or take from: sand, rock, mineral, marine growth, driftwood, fish, wildlife, agates, or souvenirs of other products of the beach lands. No fires, no tent or overnight shelter, no overnight camping . . . without permits issued by the Business Committee" of the Quinault Indian Nation, Taholah, Washington.

In Title 52.05 is provision for "physical ejection" from the reservation and possible "prosecution in the Tribal Court" for trespass without a permit. Further, equipment of trespassers "may be confiscated."

In a letter to the editor, the Business Manager stated 'Presently the Tribal Council issues very few beach use permits to persons who are not tribal members or employees. The beach closure is strictly enforced by the Tribal Trespass Patrol." He further declared, 'Reservation beaches are not open to beachcombing."

The closure is so tight that although the Washington State Highway Department has been trying to build a shortcut for Highway 101 along the beach-front between Queets and Taholah (about 15 miles) the State has not been able to complete a deal with the Tribal Office. The distance between these two points by existing state Highway 101 is about 60 miles.

Sports fishemen can obtain permits to fish Lake Quinault and along the river on the reservation, but all permits take time to obtain. The tribe has a commercial

Quinault Tribal Canoe Crafting

By arrangement with the U.S. Forest Service and the Washington State Department of Natural Resources, a giant cedar tree was selected, felled, hauled to beach site. David Forlines, carver, does the work by hand with an ax which took 9 months. Launched October 29, 1988, this sleek, 54-foot war canoe can achieve 18 knots with up to 22 paddlers, is largest recently built canoe in the world.

—Photographs by Glenn Barkhurst

Glenn Barkhurst, who lives close to the Quinault Reservation, observes the canoes in the area then hand-crafts scale models. In his words: "Quinaults use this (top) high-bow canoe to go out in ocean as well as fish from rivers. This model is 16½-inches long, about 30-feet actual size. Some canoes up to 40-feet long were to race in." The "shovelnose" double-end design (center) "I was told this was used only on the river for fishing and hunting trips." Model 17½-inches long, between 20 and 25-feet actual size. Makah tribe design (lower) with high bow for whaling expeditions at sea as well as seal hunting and fishing. On whaling trips as many as six canoes are lasted together forming a raft. The model is 14¼-inches long. Actual size varies from 20 to 28 feet.

"In all my time up here (in U.S. Coast Guard Beach Patrol unit during World War II) and seeing canoes all the time on Quileute and Quinault Rivers, I never saw a painted canoe until my return to this area in 1983." Barkhurst's models are made of white cedar and yew. He took these pictures specifically for this book.

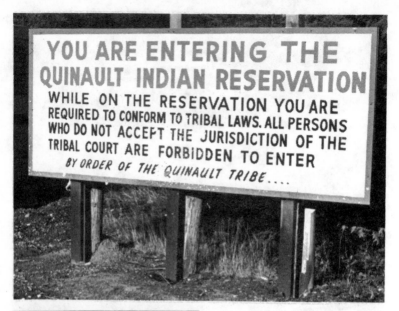

Visitors on Quinault Reservation must abide by laws of the tribe which among other things, prohibits non-Indians from beachcombing. Motor vehicles owned by the tribe mount tribal not Washington State license plates.

—Photography by Bert Webber.

cannery operating at Taholah with a retail sales outlet where its seafood items, under their trade name *Quinault Pride* are for sale.

The hand-building of cedar canoes has been a tradition of the Quinaults. These canoes are in several designs, some for use on the lake and river, others in excess of 50-feet long, are designed, and are safe for use on the ocean, often equipped with outboard motors.

Motor vehicles owned by the tribe do not carry Washington state plates, but each has a license plate embossed, 'Quinault Tribal Nation.''

Population:

1780   1,500 (Mooney, 1928; who included Quaitso)
1805   800 (Lewis and Clark, 1805-06)
1888   95 (Olson did not agree with Mooney and
              believes Mooney much too high, 800 more
              reasonable. The 1888 population is from
              Olson, who had reason to think it was
              obtained from an Indian Agent.)
1907   196 (B.I.A.—includes Quaitso)
1910   288 (U.S. Census—probably includes Quaitso)
1923   719 (Quinault Reservation—several tribes)
1937 1,200 (B.I.A.—reservation—Quinault only)
1970 1,050 (U.S. Census)
1985 2,013 (Yenne)
1987   (See Appendix)

Names by which remembered: Town on Quinault Lake (ZIP 98575); -Burn, an area once devastated by a forest fire; reservation; lake, all 3,729 acres tribal owned; river.

Sahehwamish

Linguistic group: Salishan. Nisqually dialect.

Location: Along the banks of Puget Sound and on islets in the Sound as indicated by locations of subdivisions.

Subdivisions:

Elo'sedabsh, on Medicine Creek and the lower reaches of Nisqually River, including a main settlement at the mouth of Nisqually River and Tuda'dab, at the mouth of McAllister or Medicine Creek.

Sahehwamish or Sahe'wabsh, on Shelton Inlet, including the main settlement of Sahe'wabsh, at Arcadia (post office 1874-1888, 1902-1918), and a village opposite the town of Shelton (ZIP 98584).

Skwayaithlhabsh, on Mud Bay or Eld Inlet.

Statca'sabsh, on Budd Inlet, with its principal settlement at Tumwater (ZIP 98501).

Tapi'ksdabsh, with its main settlement on Oyster Bay or Totten Inlet below the village of Oyster Bay.

Tutse'tcakl, on South Bay or Henderson Inlet, between the creek at the head and that on the south.

Population:

1780   1,200 (Mooney, 1928)
1907   780 (Mooney, 1928)

Salish (See Spokan)

Sematuse (See Spokan)

Samena
Meaning, "hunter."
Location: Around Lake Samish and on Samish Island.
This tribal name appears in Hitchman and may be related to
Samish (which see), however there is no reference to the
Samish living on the lake.

Samish
Linguistic group: Salishan.
Location: Along portions of the shore of Samish Bay;
Samish, Fidalgo, and Guemes Islands.
Villages:

> Atse'ked, on the south side of the slough at Edison on Samish
> Bay.
> Dikwi'bthl.
> Gunguna'la, on Guemes Island facing west toward Cypress
> Island.
> Hwaibathl, at Anacortes (ZIP 98221).
> Kwalo'l, at Summit Park on Fidalgo Bay.
> Nukhwhaiimikhl, on the southwest side of Guemes Island.

The name of the last village listed above is from Gibbs
(1877) and may be another name for Gunguna'la, and
Gibbs' Aseakum is perhaps Atse'ked.

Population:

> 1780   1,000 (Mooney, 1928; includes Lummi
>   and Nooksack.)
> No further counts seem to have been made.

Names by which remembered: Samish (ghost town—
post office 1871-1920); bay; island; lake; river.

Washington

Sanpoil

Also called:

> Hai-ai'-ima by the Yakima.
> Ipoilq, another Yakima name.
> Nesilextci'n, .n.selixtci'n, by Sanoil, and probably meaning 'Salish-speaking.''
> N'poch-le, a shortened form of the name.

Linguistic group: Salishan, inland division.

Location: Along Sanpoil river and along Nespelem River as well as along the Columbia River around Keller (although Keller was moved in the creation of Roosevelt Lake behind Grand Coulee Dam). Yenne places some Sanpoil in Canada.

Subdivisions and villages:

Nespelim villages:
> Haimisahun, a summer settlement of the Suspiluk, on the north bank of Columbia River about a half mile above the mouth of Nespelem River.
> Masmasalimk, home of the Smasmasalimkuwa, approximately a mile and a half above Skik.
> Nekuktshiptin, home of the Snekuktshiptimuk, at the site of the present Condon's Ferry, on the north side of the river.
> Nspilem, home of the Snspiluk, on the lower Nespelem from the falls to the mouth of the river.
> Salkuahuwithl, home of the Salkuahuwithlau, across the river from the present town of Barry (post office 1887-1940).
> Skik, home of the Skik, about a mile above Salkuahuwithl on the same side of the river.
> Skthlamchin, fishing grounds of the Salkuahuwithlau, across the river from the mouth of the Grand Coulee.
Sanpoil villages:
> Enthlukaluk, about a mile and a half north of the mouth of the river.
> Hahsulauk, home of the Shahsulauhuwa, near Plum (post office 1902-1936).
> Hulalst, home of the S-hulalstu, at Whitestone, about eight miles above Npuiluk.
> Hwatsam, a winter camp, about three miles above Snukeilt.
> Kakamkam, on the islands in the Sanpoil River a short distance above the mouth.

Kathlpuspusten, home of the Kathlpuspustenak, about a mile above Plum, on the opposite side of the river.

Ketapkunulak, on the banks of the Columbia just east of the Sanpoil River.

Naak, home of the Snaakau, about a mile below Plum but on the north side of the river.

Nhohogus, fishing grounds of the S-hulalstu.

Npokstian, a winter camp, about two miles above Hwatsam.

Npuiluk, home of the Snpuiluk, at the mouth of Sanpoil River, made up of the following camps: Snkethlkukwiliskanan, near the present landing of the Keller ferry; a branch of the last called by the same name, several hundred yards north of the first between the cliff and the Sanpoil River, on the west side; Kethltselchin, on the first bench above the Columbia, west of the Sanpoil River.

Nthlahoitk, a winter camp of the Snpuiluk, about halfway between Skthlamchin and Naak.

Saamthlk, home of the Saamthlk, on the opposite side of the river from Kathlpuspusten.

Skekwilk, on the west side of Sanpoil River about a mile above the mouth.

Snputlem, on the east bank of Sanpoil River, about an eighth of a mile above the mouth.

Snukeilt, home of the Snukeiltk, on the west side of Columbia River about one-half mile above the mouth of Spokane River.

Tkukualkuhun, home of the Stkukualkuhunak, at Rodger's Bar just across the river from Hunters (ZIP 99137).

Tsaktsikskin, a winter camp of the Snpuiluk, about a half mile below Naak.

Wathlwathlaskin, home of the Swathlwathlaskink, one-half mile up the river from Nthlahoitk.

Temporary camp sites of the Sanpoil on Sanpoil River, beginning with the first temporary camp beyond Npuiluk:

Enluhulak, about three miles above the mouth of the river.

Ksikest, on the west side of the river about halfway between the Columbia River and Keller (ZIP 99140).

Aklaiyuk, one-half mile above Ksikest.

Snkloapeten, a short distance below Keller.

Pupesten, at the present site of Keller.

Nmhoyam, about a quarter of a mile north of Keller.

Nhwiipam, a mile above Alice Creek on the east side of the river.

Seaachast, at Alice Creek.

Achhulikipastem, about half a mile north of Alice Creek.

Nliklokekuelikten, about two miles south of Cash Creek.

Nhatlchinitk, on the west side of the river at Cash Creek.

Snthulusten, on the east side of the river at the foot of a cliff, about a quarter mile above Cash Creek.

Nlupiam, one and a half miles above Snthulusten, on the same side of the river.

Slakumulemk, directly across the river from Nlupiam.

Nklakachin, on the east side of the river, at Thirty-mile Creek.

Malt, one-half mile above Thirty-mile Creek.

Lulukhum, at Devil's Elbow.

The following possible camp sites are higher upstream:

Akthlkapukwithlp, eight miles below West Fork.

Kthliipus, at the present site of Republic (ZIP 99166).

Tkwiip, near the creek at West Fork. (West Fork was a mining town in the 1890s at the confluence of the West Fork of the river and the Sanpoil River about thirteen miles south of Republic. A villager applied for a post office, but the establishing order was apparently never approved.—Ed.)

Population:

1780 800 (Mooney, 1928; however another researcher, Ray (1932), believes between 1,600 and 1,700 is more realistic. He suggests there were probably 1,300 around 1850—not unreasonable considering the large number of villages.)

1905 324 (B.I.A.—Sanpoil)
    41 (B.I.A.—Nespelem)

1910 240 (U.S. Census)

1913 202 (B.I.A.—Sanpoil)
    43 (B.I.A.—Nespelem)

Names by which remembered: Sanpoil: a lake, a river. Nespelem: City (ZIP 99155); river.

Satsop

Also called:

Sats-a-pish.

Linguistic group: Salishan

Location: Probably near the confluence of Satsop and Chehalis Rivers and upstream on the Satsop River.

Population of the Satsop seems to have been pooled with the Chehalis (which see).

1888 12 (Satsop only—Olson)

Names by which remembered: City (ZIP 98583); lakes; river; electrical power plant using nuclear energy.

Semiahmoo
Also called:

> Birch Bay Indians
> Sem-mmi-an-mas

Linguistic group: Salishan, coastal division.

Location: In the area around Semiahmoo Bay with villages on both sides of the U.S. and Canadian border. The bay is considered a length of shore rather than a "bay—an inlet of the sea," from Birch Point on the Strait of Georgia, and appears as a spit west of Blaine (ZIP 98230).

Population:

> 1843 1843 300 (Swanton)
> 1909 38 (in British Columbia. None counted in U.S.)

Names by which remembered: A bay; of historical interest as the first station in the U.S.-Canadian Boundary survey; village (post office 1872-1908).

Senijextee
Also called:

> Lake Indians

Linguistic group: Salishan. Inland division, associated with Sanpoil.

Location: Along each side of the Columbia River from about Kettle Falls into Canada as well as along the Kettle River extending to Arrow Lakes, British Columbia. The Lake Indians within the U.S. were placed on the Colville Reservation.

Population:

> 1780 500 (Mooney, 1928)
> 1909 342 (B.I.A.)
> 1910 785 (U.S. Census—with Colville)

Sinkaietk

Linguistic group: Salishan. Okanagon and Lower Okanagon dialects of interior Sakishan.

Location: Along the Okanagon River from its confluence with the Columbia River to the confluence with the Similkameen River at Oroville.

Subdivisions:

> Kartar, from the west end of Lake Omak to the Columbia River.
> Konkonelp, a winter site from about three miles above Malott (ZIP 98829) to the turn of the Okanagon River at Omak (ZIP 98841).
> Tonasket, from Riverside (ZIP 98849) upstream to Tonasket (ZIP 98855).
> Tukoratum, a winter site, from Condon's Ferry (?) on the Columbia River to the confluence with the Okanagon River then upstream to about four miles upstream of Monse (post office 1916-1962).

Population: Reported within that of the Okanagon.

Sinkakaius

Meaning: "between people."

Linguistic group: Salishan, interior division. Tribe composed mainly of people of tukoratum and the Moses Columbia bands.

Location: Between Columbia and Waterville (ZIP 98858).

No other data.

Skagit

Also called:

Hum-a-luh

Linguistic group: Salishan, coastal division.

Location: Along the Skagit and Stillaguamish Rivers. but apparently not at the rivers' mouths.

Subdivisions and villages:

> Base'lelotsed, on Skagit River from Van Horn (post office

1901-1925) to about three miles above Rockport (ZIP 98283) and Sauk River nearly to confluence with Suiattle River, includes a village, Tcagwalk, at the mouth of Sauk River.

Baska'dsadsiuk, on south bank of Skagit River from Hamilton (ZIP 98255) to Birdsview (post office 1881-1934), including a village across the river from Hamilton.

Baske'kwiuk, in Skagit River east of Rockport including a village at Marblemount (ZIP 98267) at confluence of Skagit and Cascade Rivers.

Baslo'halok, on north bank of Skagit River from Hamilton to Birdsview including a village at Hamilton.

Duwa'ha, on the drainages from South Bellingham (post office 1907-1982) to Bayview (post office 1884-1954) including along areas of Lakes Whatcom and Samish and along Samish River. Includes a village at Bayview on Padilla Bay.

Nookachamos, on Skagit River from Mount Vernon (ZIP 98273) upstream to Sedro-Woolley (ZIP 98284) and Nooka-champs River drainage, including Big Lake (post office 1898-1931), and a village east of Mount Vernon just below concrete bridge, as well as Tsa'tlabsh on Big Lake.

Sauk (post office 1886-1944), on Sauk River upstream of confluence with Suiattle River, including a village on Sauk Prairie above Darrington (ZIP 98241).

Sba'leuk, on Skagit River from above Birdsview upstream to Concrete (ZIP 98237), including a village at Concrete.

Sikwigwi'lts, on Skagit River from Sedro-Woolley upstream to just below Lyman (ZIP 98263), including a village on the flats south of Sedro-Woolley near the Skagit River.

Stillaguamish, on Stillaguamish River from Arlington (ZIP 98223) upstream including villages at Arlington and Traf-ton (post office 1889-1907).

Suiattle, on that river, including a village near the mouth of the river.

Tcubaa'bish, on Skagit River from Lyman upstream to Hamilton, including along the Day Creek drainage as well as a village at mouth of Day Creek.

Population:

1780	1,200 (Mooney, 1928; includes Swinomish)
1853	300 (Gibbs, 1877; estimated Skagit only)
1910	56 (U.S. Census)
1923	221 (B.I.A.—under name "Swinomish")
1937	200 (B.I.A.—Skagit only)
1970	259 (Yenne)
1987	(See Appendix)

Names by which remembered: A bay; ghost town (post office 1872-1904); village Skagit Head (post office April-December 1858); county; delta; island; river.

Skilloot

Linguistic group: Chinookian, Clackamas dialect

Location: Along both sides of Columbia River on each side of confluence with Cowlitz River.

Subdivisions:

> Cooniac, at Oak Point 14 miles west of Longview on Columbia River, the principal village in later times.
>
> Hullooetell, reported by Lewis and Clark, may have been a subdivision perhand Salishan.
>
> Seamysty, at mouth of Cowlitz river before 1835, probably a Skilloot band.
>
> The Thlakalama and Tlakatala of Boas (1901 and his personal information in 1905) at mouth of Kalama River about three miles upstream from Oak Point.

Population:

> 1780 3,200 (Mooney, 1928; includes 250 Thakalama)
> 1806 2,500 (Lewis and Clark)
> 1850   200 (Lane)
> After this date the tribe disappeared as an independent group.

Skin

Also called:

> Enee-shur, by Lewis and Clark

Linguistic group: Shapwailutan, Shahaptian division.

Location: Along the north bank of Columbia River from about opposite The Dalles upstream to an area opposite the Umatilla River.

Villages:

> Ka'sawi, on the Columbia opposite the mouth of Umatilla River.
>
> Skin, opposite the mouth of Deschutes River.

Uchi'chol, on the north bank of the Columbia in Klickitat
County.
Waiya'mpam, about Celilo.

Population:

1780   2,200 (Mooney, 1928; includes with Tapanash)

Snohomish
Meaning: "Tide-water people"
Also called:

Ashnuhumsh, a Kalapuyan name.

Linguistic group: Salishan, coastal division, Nisqually
dialect.
Location: Along lower Snohomish River as well as on
southern end of Whidby Island.
Subdivisions:

Sdug-wadskabsh, the south portion of Whidby Island, including
villages opposite Mukilteo (ZIP 98275) on the island
(Neg-a'sx) and at Newell (post office 1895-1904) on Useless
Bay.
Skwilsi'dia-bsh, from Preston Point above Everett (ZIP 98200)
to southern tip of Camano Island, including a village at
present Marysville (ZIP 98270) and Tcatcthlks, opposite
Tulalip (post office 1895-1953) on Tulalip Bay.
Snohomish, at Port Gardner Bay and along Snohomish River as
far upstream as Snohomish (ZIP 98290), including Tctlaks
at Everett on the south side of the mouth of the Snohomish
River and Hibolb on the north side.
Tukwet-babsh, along Snohomish River from Snohomish to
Monroe (ZIP 98272), including villages at Snohomish at
mouth of Pilchuk Creek and below Monroe two miles from
confluence of Skykomish and Snoqualmie Rivers.

Population:

1780   1,200 (Mooney, 1928; includes Snoqualmie and Tulalip)
1850   350 (Snohomish only—Swanton)
1910   664 (U.S. Census—probably includes others)
1937   667 (B.I.A.)

Snoqualmie
From: Sdo'kwalbiuq (Sdoh-kwhlb-bhuh), "not-of-much-account-but-strong."
Linguistic group: Salishan, coastal division, Nisqually dialect.
Locations:

> Skykomish, on that river above Sultan (ZIP 98294), and on the river below Goldbar (ZIP 98251).
> Snoqualmie, on that river including villages at Cherry Valley (post ffice 1878-1895), on Snoqualmie River opposite confluence of Tolt River; at Falls City (ZIP 98024), and below Snoqualmie Falls.
> Stakta'lediabsh, on Skykomish River as far up as Sultan, including Sultan Creek, including villages above Monroe at the mouth of Sultan Creek and on Sultan Creek four miles above its mouth.

Population: (See Snohomish)

1857   225 (Swanton)

Names by which remembered: City (ZIP 98065); falls; Snoqualmie Falls (ZIP 98066); lake; mountain; national forest; pass; Snoqualmie Little Sister (mountain).

Spokan
Also called:

> Lêcle'cuks, Wasco name probably intended for this tribe.
> Lar-ti-e-lo, by Lewis and Clark in 1806.
> Sɛnoxami'naɛx, by the Okanagon, from their principal division.
> Sɛntutu' or Sɛnoxma'n, by the Upper Kutenai from the Salish names for the Middle and Little Spokan respectively.

Linguistic group: Salishan, inland division. Most closely connected with Kalispel, Pend d'Oreilles, Sematuse, Salish.
Location: Along Spokane and Little Spokane Rivers, south to Cow Creek and north to include all feeder streams of the Spokane River.

Subdivisions: The Lower Spokan (about the mouth and on the lower part of Spokane River, including the present Spokane Indian Reservation); Upper Spokan or Little Spokan (occupying the valley of the Little Spokane River and all the country east of the lower Spokane to within the borders of Idaho); the South or Middle Spokan (occupying at least the lower part of Hangmans Creek, extending south along the borders of the Skitswish).

History: Researchers fairly well agree that the Spokans are a mix of many tribes which, over time, discovered the good living in the vicinity of Spokane Falls (now in the center of the city of Spokane) and a little downstream at the confluence with the Spokane and Little Spokane Rivers. Looking at weather conditions alone, the area around Davenport about 35 miles west is semi-arid—very little rain—while rainfall at Coeur d'Alene at the base of the Bitterroot Mountains, about 35 miles east of Spokane, is heavy. The blessing of living in Spokane, at the mid-point of these extremes, is as obvious to people today as it surely was to native Americans a few hundred years ago.

There were serious battles between settlers and Indians around Spokane which included the Battle of Four Lakes. In decisive running warfare just east of Rosalia, the Indians trounced the cavalry of Colonel Edward J. Steptoe. The followup punitive expedition headed by Colonel George Wright would win the war, but only after ruthless measures against the Indians. The Colonel ordered the killing of hundreds of the Indians' horses, then he burned all their foodstuffs. He hanged seven Indians on an Indian council ground near Sin-sin-too-ooley ("place where little fish are caught") Creek, which the settlers promptly labeled Hangman's Creek, then established a postoffice by that name (1873-1881), renamed Alpha (1881-1883), present name Latah (ZIP 98018). As the state legislature didn't like the name Hangman's Creek, or the event that caused the use of that name, a Bill was passed changing the name to Latah Creek. Even to this writing, however, many locals still refer to this stream as Hangman's Creek.

Some say it was "Divine Retribution" that brought about

the death of Colonel Wright. He was a passenger on the steamer *Brother Jonathan* when the ship, pounded by monstrous seas, struck St. George Reef off Crescent City, California, on July 30, 1865. Of the 185 persons aboard only 19 were saved—Colonel Wright not among the rescued. (Fort George Wright, on the western edge of Spokane, was named for him. Colonel Steptoe is remembered by Steptoe Butte and Steptoe Butte State Park [elevation 3,673] in Whitman County. The butte had been used as a lookout post for both the Indians and the army.)

The Pacific Northwest Indian Center is a major museum and research library dealing with Indians of the area. The museum is not far from Gonzaga University in Spokane.

After settlement and treaty, the Spokan Indians were sent to the Colville and Flathead Reservations.

Population:

1780	1,400 (Mooney, 1928; but Teit claims 2,500)
1806	600 (Lewis and Clark, but Swanton suggests this number is a guess)
1905	277 (B.I.A.—Lower Spokan on Spokane Reservation)
	177 (B.I.A.—Middle and Upper Spokan on Colville Reservation)
	135 (B.I.A.—Flathead Reservation)
1909	509 (B.I.A.—Spokane Reservation)
	138 (B.I.A.—Flathead Reservation)
1910	443 (U.S. Census)
1923	669 (B.I.A.)
1937	847 (B.I.A.)
1970	1,500 (B.I.A.—Spokane Reservation)
1985	1,961 (B.I.A.—Spokane Reservation)
1987	(See Appendix)

Names by which remembered: City (ZIP 99200); Air Force Base renamed Fairchild AFB; Spokane Bridge, town (post office 1867-1958); county; falls; Spokane Falls, town (post office 1872-1891); Reservation; battlefield; river.

Squaxon (Squakson)
Also called:

Skwak-sin, Indian name.

Linguistic group: Salishan, coastal division, Nisqually dialect.
Location: North Bay, at extreme east end of Hood Canal about 12 miles southwest of Bremerton (ZIP 98310) and near present town of Allyn (ZIP 98524).
Villages:

At mouth of Coulter Creek and North Bay.
At mouth of Mason Creek at Allyn.

Population:

1780   1,000 (Mooney, 1928—with other tribes)
1909   98 (Swanton)
1937   32 (Swanton)

Squamish
Also called:

Suk-wa-bish

Linguistic group: Salishan, Nisqually branch of coastal division.
Location: Along the west shore of Puget Sound claiming as territory all areas between Applegate Cove and Gig Harbor.
Subdivisions and villages:

Saktabsh, on Sinclair Inlet, Dyes Inlet and at Blakeley (post office 1884-1886, 1907-1908); on Eagle Harbor (post office 18677-1890).
Suquamish (ZIP 98392) on Liberty Bay, at Port Madison (post office 1858-1943), and at Point Monroe.

Population:

1857 441 (Swanton)
1909 180 (Swanton)
1910 307 (U.S. Census)
        204 (B.I.A.—with Squamish)
1937 168 (B.I.A.)

Names by which remembered: Town in which Chief Sealth ("Chief Seattle") is buried.

Swallah
Also called:

Swalash

Location: In the San Juan Islands on Orcas Island and on San Juan Island.
Villages:

Hutta'tchl, on the southeast end of Orcas Island (ZIP 98280).
Klala'kamish, on the east side of San Juan Island.
Lemaltcha, on Waldron Island (ZIP 98297).
Stashum, on Waldron Island.

No further data.

Swinomish
Linguistic group: Salishan, coastal division. Sometimes referred to as a subdivision of Skagit.
Location: Northern end of Whidby Island and around the mouth of Skagit River.
Subdivisions and villages:

Ho'baks, on the upper end of Penn's Cove, not far from San de Fuca (post office 1890-1954).
Batsa'dsali, at Coupeville (ZIP 98239); Ba'asats between Coupeville and Snaklem Point west of Long Point, and Tcubaa'ltced on the north side of Snaklem Point about four miles from Coupeville.
Kikia'los, on Skagit Bay from the South Fork of Skagit River to the north tip of Camano Island (post office 1959-1969), with a village at the mouth of Carpenter Creek between Conway (ZIP 98238), and Fir (post office 1880-1932), and

another called Atsala'di at Utsalady (post office 1865-1910) on Camano Island.

Kwa'dsakbiuk, on the lower reaches of Stillaguamish River and Port Susan, with a village at the mouth of the Stillaguamish.

Skagit, on Whidbey Island, from Oak Harbor (ZIP 97277), south to Snaklem Point, with a village at Oak Harbor.

Skwada'bsh, on the North Fork of the Skagit River and the eastern part of Whidbey Island lying north of Oak Harbor, with Skwi'kwikwab at the mouth of the North Fork of the Skagit, and Tcotab on a point across Skagit Bay.

Swinomish, on southern Padilla Bay, Swinomish Slough which joins Padilla Bay and Skagit Bay, Skagit Bay from Sullivan Slough north, and the southeast portion of Fidalgo Island, with the following villages: Kalekut (not far from Whitney at the highway bridge), Sde'os (near Lone Tree Point), Shuptada'tci (on Swinomish Slough three miles from La Conner), and another village (on Sullivan Slough just east of La Conner [ZIP 98257]).

Population: Enumeration includes Skagit (which see).

Names by which remembered: Channel (navigation); Reservation; village later renamed La Conner.

Taidnapum

Also called:

Upper Cowlitz

Linguistic group: Shapwailutan. Shahaptian division.

Location: Near headwaters of Cowlitz River with some extension to the Lewis River.

Population:

1780 600 (Mooney, 1928; includes Klickitat)
Not enumerated separately after 1907.

Tapanash (See Skin)

Twana

Means: "portage"

Also called:

Tu-a'd-hu, own name.
Skokomish, from the name of a principal division.
Wi'lfa Ampa'fa ami'm, Luckiamute-Kalapuya name.

Linguistic group: Salishan, coastal division.
Location: Along both sides of Hood Canal. During the period of relocation to reservations this tribe took up residence on Skokomish Reservation.
Subdivisions and villages:

Kolsid, on Quilcene (ZIP 98376) Bay and on Dabop Bay.
Skokomish (post office 1858-1890), around Annas Bay and the lower Skokomish River.
Soatlkobsh, both sides of Hood Canal from Seabeck (ZIP 98380) and Oak Head to Port Gamble (ZIP 98364), and Squamish (post office 1905, 1907-1908, 1908-1909) Harbor.
Habha'b, at Eldon (post office 1901-1925) on Hood Canal at mouth of Hammermammer River.
Li'liwap, at lilliwap (ZIP 98555) on Hood Canal.
Skoko'bsh, at mouth of Skokomish River.
Tule'lalap, on the eastern end of the canal at mouth of Mission Creek.
Two villages at Duckabush (post office 1891-1926) and Brinnon (ZIP 98320).

Population:

1780	1,000 (Mooney, 1928; includes Skokomish and Squaxon)
1853	265 (Swanton)
1910	61 (U.S. Census—Twana)
	195 (U.S. Census—Skokomish)
1937	206 (B.I.A.)

Names by which remembered: A state park.

Wallawalla
Meaning: "little river"
Also called:

Walula

Linguistic group: Shapwailutan, Shahaptian division. Closely related to Nez Perce.

The Vanishing Wanapums

The tribe of peaceful and religious people has dwindled to a single full-blood member, Bobby Tomanawash (right). Others shown, Frank Buck, died July 10, 1988 and Rex Buck (center) died in 1975. In early 1989 the Grant County Public Utilities District No. 2 signed a new agreement with the Wanapums concerning the operation of Priest Rapids and Wanapum dams on the Columbia River. Representing the tribe are only 15 adults "and a number of minor children." The Wanapums live in Wanapum Village near Priest Rapids.

—Photo courtesy Grant County PUD No. 2

Location: Along lower Walla Walla River other than the area occupied by Cayuse near ghost town of Whitman (post office 1870-1875) and present Whitman Mission National Historic Site, and a short area along the Columbia River and Snake River near their confluence. The tribe was moved to Umatilla Reservation.

Population:

1780	1,500 (Mooney, 1928; includes Umatilla)
1805	1,600 (Lewis and Clark estimate, which included others
1910	397 (U.S. Census)
1923	628 (B.I.A.)
1937	631 (B.I.A.)
1987	(See Appendix)

Names by which remembered: City (ZIP 00362); early fort; county, river.

Wanapam

Linguistic group: Shapwailutan, Shahaptian division, close association with Palouse.

Location: Along the Columbia River between Priest Rapids and just below Umatilla River confluence. Some villages, plausibly just seasonal hunting stations, east of Pasco.

The tribe may have been in two divisions:

Chamnapum
Wanapam

History: Hitchman pointed out that the tribal name means "the river people" and states the tribe at one time numbered 3,000, but only eight remained at his time of writing. The Wanapams never had a treaty with the U.S. Government apparently because these Indians were never at war, so the government had no reason for a treaty. With no treaty, no reservation.

Population:

1780   1,800 (Mooney, 1928)

1985   6 (Editor's interview with one of the six at
                Interpretative Center, Wanapam Dam)

Names by which remembered: Wanapam Dam, reservoir; interpretative center on Columbia River.

Watlala (See Oregon)

Wauyukma
Linguistic group: Shapwailutan, Shahaptian division. Closely related to Palouse.
Location: Along the Snake River downstream from confluence with Palouse River.
Population: Unknown. (See Palouse)

Wenatchee (Wina't.ca)
    Also called:

> Awena'tchela, by the Klickitat, meaning "people at the coming-out or source," said to refer to the fact that they occupied the country at the heads of the rivers or above the Yakima River.
> Pisquow, from .s.npeskwu'zux, their own name, variants of which appear in the appelations given them by other Salish tribes in the neighborhood.
> Tso'kwob.c, by the Snohomish.
> Wahnahchee, by Lewis and Clark.

Linguistic group: Salishan, inland divivion.
Subdivisions:

> Sinia'lkumuk, on the Columbia between Entiat Creek and Wenatchee River.
> Sinkumchi'muk, at the mouth of the Wenatchee River.
> Sinpusko'isok, at the forks of the Wenatchee, where the town of Leavenworth (ZIP 98826) now stands.
> Sintia'tkumuk, along Entiat Creek.
> Stske'tamihu, six miles down river from the present town of Wenatchee (ZIP 98801).
> Camiltpaw, on the east side of Columbia River.
> Shanwappom, on the headwaters of Cataract (Klickitat) and Tapteel Rivers.

Siapkat, at a place of this name on the east bank of Columbia
River, about Bishop Rock and Milk Creek, below Wenatchee River.

Skaddal, originally on Cataract (Klickitat) River, on the west
bank of Yakima River and later opposite the entrance to
Selah Creek.

Location: Along Methow River, Wenatchee River and
Lake Chelan.
Population:

1780	1,400 (Mooney, 1928)
1805	820 (Lewis and Clark)
1910	52 (U.S. Census)

Names by which remembered: City (ZIP 98801); creek;
lake; national forest; mountain pass; mountain ridge; state
park.

Wishram
Also called:

E-che-loot, by Lewis and Clark in 1806, from their their own
name.
Ila'xluit, their own name and from this called Tlakluit.
Wu'cxam, by the Yakima and Klickitats

Linguistic group: Chinookian.
Location: Along the north side of Columbia River in
Klickitat County.
Villages:

Atatathlia itcagitkok, on a small island near Celilo Falls, or
more likely Ten-Mile Rapids.
Chalaitgelit, a short distance east of The Dalles.
Gawilapchk, a winter village below The Dalles.
Gawishila, a fishing station above The Dalles.
Hladakhat, about 10 miles below The Dalles.
Hliluseltshlikh, below Big Eddy.
Kwalasints, opposite The Dalles.
Nayakkhachikh, a winter village below Gawilapchk.
Niukhtash, at Big Eddy.
Shabanahksh, one mile below Wishram (?) (ZIP 98673).

Shgwaliksh, perhaps Klickitat, about 12 miles (?) below The
Dalles.
Shikeldaptikh, about a half mile below The Dalles.
Shkagech, below Crate's Point.
Shkonana, opposite Crate's Point.
Shkukskhat, below The Dalles.
Tsapkhadidlit, a wintering place below Nayakkhachikh.
Waginkhak, below The Dalles and the lowest Tlakluit town on
the river.
Wakemap, above Wishram.
Wasnaniks, below Skukskhat.
Wayagwa, above The Dalles, the easternmost town.
Wishram (properly called Nixlúidix), about five miles above
The Dalles.

History: There was a more-or-less permanent village in
vicinity of today's town where the Indians maintained a
trading post to which inland tribes sent their goods to
exchange with the tribes from down-river. This village was
just upriver from the great Celilo Falls fishing grounds.
Population:

1780   1,500 (Mooney, 1928)
1800   1,000 (Spier, 1930)
1806   1,000 (Lewis and Clark, 1805-06)
1910   274 (U.S. Census)
1937   124 (B.I.A., listed as "Upper Chinook")

Names by which remembered: Town (ZIP 98673).

Wynoochee
Linguistic group: Salishan, coastal division. Related to
Chehalis.
Location: Along Wynoochee River and at confluence
with Chehalis at Montesano (ZIP 98563).
No other data.

Yakima
Meaning: "runaway."
Also called:

Cuts-sáh-nem, by Clark in 1805 in Lewis and Clark Journals
(1804-5).

186

Pa'kiut'lema, own name, "people of the gap."

Shanwappoms, from Lewis and Clark in 1805.

Stobshaddat, by the Puget Sound tribes, meaning "robbers."

Waptai'lmin, own name, "people of the narrow river." Both of their names for themselves refer to the narrows in Yakima River at Union Gap (ZIP 98903), where their chief village was situated.

Linguistic group: Shapwailutal, Shahaptian division.
Location: Along the banks of the lower Yakima River.
Subdivisions:

Atanum-lema, on Atanum Creek.

Nakchi'sh-hlama, on Naches River, and hence possibly Pshwa'nwapam.

Pisko, about the mouth of Toppenish Creek.

Se'tas-lema, on Satus Creek.

Si'-hlama, on Yakima River above the mouth of Toppenish Creek.

Si'la-hlama, on Yakima River between Wenas and Umtanum Creeks.

Si'mkoe-hlama, on Simcoe Creek.

Tkai'waichash-hlama, on Cowiche Creek.

Topinish, on Toppenish Creek.

Waptailmin, at or below Union Gap.

It is quite possible that under the term "Yakima" several distinct tribes were included.

History: Lewis and Clark mention these Indians and used the name "Cutsahnim" for them. The term is presumed to have included various other bands probably never separately identified.

The United States made a treaty in 1855 with the Yakima as well as 13 other tribes. The treaty called for the Indians to give up all their land from the Palouse and Snake River area to Lake Chelan, to the Cascade Mountains and to the Columbia River in exchange for the Yakima Reservation. Chief Kamaiakan was to be leader of the confederation on the reservation. However, before the ratification of this treaty, the Yakima Indian War started, thus it took four years before the terms of the treaty would be worked out. Some tribes, including the Palouse, refused to sign (see Palouse) and never took up reservation residence.

The name "Yakima" is currently used to describe the confederation of Native Americans within the area of the reservation, thus it seems unlikely that pure-blood Yakimas exist. If so, they do not seem to be enumerated separately.

Population:

1780	3,000 (Mooney, 1928)
1806	1,200 (Lewis and Clark, 1805-06)
1910	1,362 (U.S. Census)
1923	2,939 (B.I.A.)
1937	2,933 (B.I.A.)
1950	3,370 (Yenne)
1970	5,392 (Yenne)
1985	7,987 (B.I.A.—Yakima Reservation)
1987	(See Appendix)

Names by which remembered: The designation of the name "Yakima" to define the large group of tribes assembled on the reservation. City (ZIP 98900); county; creek; falls; peak; park; river; state park.

APPENDIX A

Unique Subjects Casual Readers May Have Missed

1. This Indian war seen "live" on TV (1973)
                          See: Nebraska, Sioux
2. Indian buried with full military funeral
                          See: Wyoming, Shoshoni
3. Sedentary tribe migrated, split, at war with neighbors, resumed sedentary life on reservation
                          See: Wyoming, Arapaho
4. Indian Chief who lived to age 96
                          See: Wyoming, Shoshoni
5. The vegetable that caused a war
                          See: Idaho, Bannock
6. Quotation: "I will fight no more forever"
                          See: Idaho, Nez Perce
7. How the telegraph won a war
                          See: Idaho, Nez Perce
8. Church that gave its land to a tribe (1988)
                          See: Oregon, Klamath
9. Indian Chief whose head was sent to Wash. D.C.
                          See: Oregon, Modoc
10. Tribe responsible for Whitman Massacre
                          See: Oregon, Cayuse
11. National Guard summer camp named for
                          See: Oregon, Clatsop
12. Minister who regularly preached to a congregation of 1
                          See: Oregon, Klamath
13. Probably the most costly Indian war
                          See: Oregon, Modoc
14. Tribe that operates summer resort (Kah-Nee-Ta)
                          See: Oregon, Warm Springs

15. Common trade language used by Indians/traders
> See: Oregon, Chinook
16. Massacre at the Cascades of the Columbia
> See: Washington, Klickitat
17. Indians fight the Spanish
> See: Washington, Quinault
18. Whites are forbidden to beachcomb or walk the beach
> See: Washington, Quinault
19. They build canoes that will do up to 18 knots in the ocean
> See: Washington, Quinault
20. Tribe with a single full-blood member living as this book goes to press
> See: Washington, Quinault

APPENDIX B

Indian Populations for January 1987
Bureau of Indian Affairs

Statistics provided are limited to those for the states covered in this book. A comprehensive report for all states is available from the Bureau of Indian Affairs. The data on populations presented here are not intended as exhaustive as such thoroughness appears unavailable even to the Bureau of Indian Affairs. The B.I.A. asserts, "Accuracy varies from place to place."—*Indian Service Population and Labor Force Estimates,* B.I.A., January 1987.

Definitions and Coverage

"Indian" is defined as a person who is a member, of one-fourth degree or more blood quantum descendant of a member, of any Indian tribe. "Indian tribe" is any Indian tribe, band, nation, rancheria, pueblo, colony, or community including Alaska Native villages as defined in the Alaska Native Claims Act (85 Stat. 688). "Resident Indian" is an Indian living *on* Federal Reservations or *nearby* who are considered part of the service population of the bureau of Indian Affairs. "Nearby" is defined as those areas adjacent or contiguous to Reservations. The limits of what is considered part of the service population of the Bureau of Superintendent with recommendations from tribal governing bodies. Indians in these "nearby" areas meet general criteria which includes a written designation of the tribal governing body that members of their tribe, and family members who are Indian, residing in the area are socially, culturally, and economically affiliated with their tribe and Reservation and are in geographical proximity of the

191

Reservation. Further, the "nearby" area is in suitable proximity to the Reservation to assure adequate level of services.

Statistics shown refer to population of a *geographic area and not to tribal membership*. Rules for who may be a member of a specific tribe are determined by each tribe and may include members living in widely separated areas. Many of the data are estimates originating in local Agency offices of Bureau of Indian Affairs from whatever information may be available for the Reservation or tribal entity. Accuracy varies from place to place. Accuracy can be very good at small isolated locations where everyone's activity is common knowledge. But for large areas, such as Alaska and the Navajo Reservation (neither in this book) data are, in the words of the B.I.A. "expensive to collect and are often subject to considerable errors." While many of the numbers reported are estimates from local offices, the numbers are presented "as is" and not rounded. Small numbers when rounded might totally disappear from the study.

POPULATIONS BY STATE (ESTIMATES)

	B.I.A. TOTAL	65 & OVER	UNDER 16	16 & OVER
Nebraska	3,928	178	1,521	2,407
Wyoming	5,124	261	1,478	3,646
Idaho	7,495	496	2,274	5,221
Oregon	7,180	435	2,403	4,777
Washington	40,486	1,775	14,532	25,954

POPULATIONS LIVING ON OR ADJACENT TO RESERVATIONS

Winnebago Agency Nebraska
Omaha Reservation:

2,037	66	845	1,192

Santee Sioux Reservation:

519	31	194	325

	B.I.A. TOTAL	65 OVER	UNDER 16	16 & OVER
Wind River Agency Wyoming				
Wind River Reservation:				
Includes Arapaho and Shoshoni				
	5,124	261	1,478	3,646
Fort Hall Agency Idaho				
Fort Hall Reservation:				
	3,655	244	1,125	2,530
Northern Idaho Agency				
Coeur d'Alene Reservation:				
	939	57	235	704
Kootenai Reservation:				
	118	1	35	83
Nez Perce Reservation:				
	2,455	161	784	1,671
Siletz Agency Oregon				
Coos Bay Tribes:				
Appears in this compilation for the first time				
	221	11	64	157
Cow Creek Tribes:				
	408	28	136	272
Grand Ronde Tribes:				
Appears in this compilation for the first time				
	1,044	169	221	823
Siletz Reservation:				
	1,257	44	360	897
Umatilla Agency Oregon				
Umatilla Reservation:				
	1,610	90	603	1,007
Warm Springs Agency Oregon				
Burns-Paiute Colony:				
	216	13	75	141
Warm Springs Reservation:				
	2,424	80	944	1,480
Colville Agency Washington				
Colville Reservation:				
	3,868	243	1,337	2,531

	B.I.A. TOTAL	65 & OVER	UNDER 16	16 & OVER
Olympic Peninsula Agency Washington				
Chehalis Reservation:	742	46	264	478
Hoh Reservation:	97	2	40	57
Jamestown Klallam Tribe:	377	54	91	286
Lower Elwah Reservation:	1,059	26	430	629
Makah Reservation:	953	45	358	595
Quileute Reservation:	495	9	136	359
Quinault Reservation:	2,055	76	755	1,300
Shoalwater Reservation:	94	9	30	64
Skokomish Reservation:	829	28	306	523
Squaxin Island Reservation:	1,186	38	388	798
Puget Sound Agency Washington				
Lummi Island Reservation:	2,888	172	1,249	1,639
Muckleshoot Reservation:	2,793	112	1,145	1,648
Nisqually Reservation:	1,455	87	609	846
Nooksack Tribe:	956	66	458	498
Port Gamble Reservation:	612	20	151	461
Port Madison Reservation:	652	44	225	427
Puyallup Reservation:	7,680	203	2,611	4,069
Sauk-Suiattle Reservation:	210	8	55	155
Stillagumamish Reservation:	484	14	203	281

Appendix B

	B.I.A. TOTAL	65 & OVER	UNDER 16	16 & OVER
Swinomish Reservation:	633	43	203	430
Tulalip Reservation:	1,408	41	684	724
Upper Skagit Tribe:	370	24	108	262
Spokane Agency Washington				
Kalispel Reservation:	258	5	102	156
Spokane Reservation:	1,486	92	515	971
Yakima Agency Washington				
Yakima Reservation:	6,846	268	2,079	4,767

BIBLIOGRAPHY

Amsler, Melba, *et al. Facts & Fancy of Uinta County's Past [Wyoming]*. Uinta County Museum, Evanston. n.d.

Babcock, Chester and Clare A. Babcock. *Our Pacific Northwest Yesterday and Today*. McGraw-Hill. 1963

Barrett, S.A. *The Material Culture of the Klamath and Modoc Indians*. University of California Publications American Archaeological and Ethnological, Vol. 5, No. 4, pp. 239-292. 1910

Berreman, Joel V. *Tribal Distribution in Oregon*. [Memorial, American Anthropological Association, No. 47.] Smithsonian. 1937

Boardman, Tim and Richard W. Helbock. *Washington Post Offices*. Raven. 1986

Boas, Franz. "Tsimishian Mythology." *31st Annual Report* [Bureau of American Ethnology 1909-1910] pp. 29-1037. 1916

_____. "The Ethnology of the Kwakiutl, Based on Data Collected by George Hunt." *35th Annual Report* [Bureau of American Ethnology 1913-1914] pp. 43-794. 1921

_____. Map showing the distribution of Salish tribes and their neighbors about the end of the 18th century. (Accompanying a paper on "Sound Shifts in Salishan Dialects," by Franz Boas and Herman Haeberlin. *International Journal of American Linguistics*. Vol. 4. Nos. 2-4.) N.Y. 1927

Boas, Franz and James Teit. *Coeur d'Alene. Flathead and Okanogan Indians*. [Smithsonian Institution Bureau of American Ethnology 45th Report 1927-1928] YeGalleon. 1985

Boone, Lilia. *Idaho Place Names*. Univ. of Idaho Press. 1987

Burns, Robert I. S.J. *The Jesuits and the Indian Wars of the Northwest*. Yale. 1966

California; A Guide to the Golden State. Federal Writers Project W.P.A. Hastings. 1967

Cannon, Miles. *Waiilatpu, Its Rise and Fall*. YeGalleon. 1969

Catlin, George. *Letters and Notes on the Manners and Customs and Condition of the North American Indians*. 2 vols. New York and London. 1844

Chalmers II, Harvey. *The Last Stand of the Nez Perce*. Twayne. 1962

Colorado, A Guide to the Highest State. Federal Writer's Project. W.P.A. 1949

Corning, Howard M. *Dictionary of Oregon History*. Binford. 1956

Costello, J.A. *The Siwash; Their Life Legends and Tales*. [1895] YeGalleon. 1986

Cressman, Luther S. *The Sandal and the Cave*. Oregon State University Press. 1981

Cross, Osborne. *A Report in the form of a Journal, March of the Regiment of Mounted Riflemen to Oregon in 1849*. [1851] YeGalleon. 1967

Curtis, Edward S. *The North American Indian*. 14 vols. (1, Apache, Jicarillas, Navaho; 2, Pima, Papago, Qahatika, Yuma, Maricopa, Walapai, Havasupai,

Bibliography

Apache-Mohave; 3, Teton Sioux, Yanktonai, Assiniboin; 4, Apsaroke, Hidatsa; 5, Mandan, Arikara, Atsina; 6, Piegan, Cheyenne, Arapaho; 7, Yakima, Klickitat, Interior Salish, Kutenai; 8, Nez Percés, Wallawalla, Umatilla, Cayuse, Chinookan tribes; 9, Salishan tribes of the Coast, Chimakum, Quilliute, Wallapa; 10, the Kwakiutl;p 11, Nootka, Haida; 12, the Hopi; 13, Klamath; 14, Kato, Wailaki, Yuki, Pomo, Mintun, Maidu, Yokuts.) New York. 1907-1930

Depradations and Massacre by the Snake River Indians. Exec. Doc. No. 46. 36th Cong. 2nd Session. House of Representatives. 1861. (Reprinted YeGalleon. 1966)

DeSmet, Pierre-Jean, S.J. *New Indian Sketches.* YeGalleon. 1985

DeVoto, Bernard (ed). *The Journals of Lewis and Clark.* Houghton Mifflin. 1953

Eells, Myron. "The Twana Indians of the Skokomish Reservation in Washington Territory." *Bull. U.S. Beol. and Geogr. Surv.,* vol. 3, Nol. 1. 1877
The Twana, Chemakum, and Klallam Indians of Washington Territory. Ann. Rep. Smithsonian Inst. for 1887, pp. 605-681. 1889

Fisher, Vardis, *Encyclopedia of Idaho.* Federal Writer's Project W.P.A. Caxton. 1938

Forney, Jacob. "United States Office of Indian Affairs." *Report,* p. 213. 1858

Franzwa, Gregory M. *Maps of the Oregon Trail.* The Patrice Press. 1982
_____. *The Oregon Trail Revisited.* The Patrice Press. (3rd ed) 1983

Gallagher, John S. and Alan H. Patera. *Wyoming Post Offices 1850-1980.* The Depot. 1980

Ghent, W.J. *The Road to Oregon; A Chronicle of the Great Emigrant Trail.* Longmans, Green. 1929

Gibbs, George. *Indian Tribes of Washington Territory.* [1855] YeGalleon. 1978

Gibbs, James A. *Shipwrecks of the Pacific Coast.* Binford. 1962

Haines, Aubrey. *Historic Sites Along the Oregon Trail.* The Patrice Press. (2nd ed) 1985

Hale, Horatio. *Ethnology and Philology.* U.S. Exploring Exped. 1836-1842, under command of Charles Wilkes, U.S.N., vol. 6. Philadelphia. 1846

Heckert, Elizabeth. *The People and the River; A History of the Takilma Indians of the Upper Rogue River Country.* (private print) 1977

Helbock, Richard W. *Oregon Post Offices 1847-1982.* LaPosta. 1982

Hepner, Br. Simon. *Hardships on the Oregon Trail.* (A paper for the fulfillment of a degree at Mt. Angel Abbey.) 1977

Hitchman, Robert. *Place Names of Washington.* Wash. State Hist. Society. 1985

Hodge, Frederick Webb. *Handbook of American Indians North of Mexico.* [Smithsonian Institution Bureau of Americna Ethnology Bulletin 30, 1905] Rowman. 1965

Howe, Carrol B. *Ancient Modocs of California and Oregon.* Binford. 1979
_____. *Ancient Tribes of Klamath County.* Binford. 1968

Iberville, Pierre la Moyne d'. *See:* Margry, Pierre.

Indians Along the Oregon Trail

Indians Along the Oregon Trail

Idaho, a Guide in Word and Picture. Federal Writer's Project. W.P.A. Caxton. 1937

"Indian Affairs [of the United States]." Office of Indian Affairs, War Department. *Reports.* 1825-1848. Report of the Commissioner, Department of the Interior, 1849-1932. In Report of the Department of the Interior, 1933—.

Johnson, Olga W. *Flathead and Kootenay; the Rivers, the Tribes and the Region's Traders.* Clark. 1969.

Jones, Peter. *History of the Ojebway [Chippawa]; with Especial References to their Conversion to Christianity.* London. 1861

Kasner, Leone Letson. *Siletz; Survival for an Artifact.* Itemizer-Observer. 1977

Kroeber, Alfred L. "Shoshonean Dialects of California." *University of California Publication of American Archaeology and Ethnology.* Vol. 4, No. 3. 1907

_____. "The Religion of the Indians of California." *University of California Publications of American Archaeology and Ethnology.* Vol. 4. pp. 319-356. 1907

_____. "Cultural and Natural Areas of Native North America." *University of California Publications on American Archaeology and Ethnology.* Vol. 38. 1939

Landrum, Francis S. *Guardhouse, Gallows and Graves.* Klamath County Museum Foundation, Klamath Falls, Oreg. 1988

Lane, Joseph. "Report of United States Office of Indian Affairs for 1850." (War Department) p. 161. 1850

Lee, Daniel and Joseph Frost. *Ten Years in Oregon.* YeGalleon. 1968

Lewis, Meriwether, and William Clark. *The Journal of Lewis and Clark, to the Mouth of the Columbia River Beyond the Rocky Mountains.* Dayton, Ohio. 1840

Lowdon, Mildred. *The Klamath Tribe.* Klamath County [Oregon] League of Women Voters. 1974

Margry, Pierre. *Découvertes et établissements des Francais dans l'ouest et dans le sud de l'Amérique Septentrionale (1614-1754).* Mémoires et documents originaux. Pts. 1-6. Paris. Vol. 4, p. 514. 1875-1886

Mattes, Merrill J. *The Great Platte River Road.* Nebraska State Hist. Society. 1969

Miller, Emma G. *Clatsop County, Oregon; A History.* Binfords. 1958

Mooney, James. *The Ghost-dance Religion and the Sioux Outbreak of 1890.* [14th Annual Report Bureau of American Ethnology, 1892-93. pt. 2, pp. 641-1110.] Smithsonian. 1896

_____. *Calendar History of the Kiowa Indians.* [17th Annual Report Bureau of American Ethnology, 1895-1896. pt. 1. pp. 129-445.] Smithsonian. 1898

_____. *The Cheyenne Indians.* [Memorial, American Anthropological Association, Vol. 1, pt. 6.] Smithsonian. 1907

_____. *The Aboriginal Population of America North of Mexico.* Smithsonian Miscel. Collection. Vol. 80, No. 7. 1928

Mullan, John. *Report on the Indian Tribes in the Eastern Portion of Washington Territory, 1853.* Pacific Railroad Reports. Vol. 1. pp. 437-441. Washington, D.C. 1855

Murdock, George Peter. *Ethnographic Bibliography of North America.* [Dept. of Anthropology] Yale Univ. Press. 1941

198

Bibliography

Murie, James R. *Pawnee Indian Societies.* [Anthropologic Papers] Museum of Natural History. vol. 11, pp. 543-644. Washington, D.C. 1914

McArthur, Lewis A. *Oregon Geographic Names.* Oreg. Hist. Society Press. (4th Ed) 1974

Nebraska; A Guide to Cornhuskers State. Federal Writer's Project. W.P.A. Sommerset. 1974

Neils, Selma. *The Klickitat Indians.* Binford. 1985

The New Washington; A Guide to the Evergreen State. Federal Writer's Project. W.P.A. Binford. 1941 (Rev. Ed. 1950)

Nicandri, David L. *Northwest Chiefs.* Wash. State Hist. Society. 1984

Ogden, Peter Skene. *Traits of American Indian Life.* Grabhorn. 1933

Oregon End of the Trail. Federal Writer's Project. W.P.A. Binford. 1940

The Oregon Trail; Missouri River to the Pacific Ocean. Federal Writer's Project. W.P.A. Hastings. 1939

Parker, Samuel. *Journal of an Exploring Tour Beyond the Rocky Mountains.* Ithaca, 1838, 1840, 1842, 1846. (*See:* 1840 vol., p. 257.) 1840

Peterson, Emil R. and Alfred Powers. *A Century of Coos and Curry [Counties].* Binford. 1952

Ray, Verne F. "The Sanpoil and Nespelem: Salishan Peoples of Northeastern Washington." *Univ. Washington Publ. Anthrop.,* vol. 5, Dec. 1932. Seattle. 1932

_____. "Lower Chinook Ethnographic Notes." *Univ. Washington Publ. Anthrop.,* vol. 7, No. 2, pp. 29-165. Seattle. 1938

Ray, Verne F., *et al.* "Tribal distribution in eastern Oregon and adjacent regions." *Amer. Anthrop.,* n. s., vol. 40, No. 3, pp. 384-415. (Containing: "Tribal distribution in northeastern Oregon," by Verne F. Ray, pp. 384-395; "Notes on the Tenino, Molala, and Paiute of Oregon," by George Peter Murdock, pp. 395-402; "Northern Paiute," by Omer C. Stewart, pp. 405-407; "Western Shoshoni," by Jack Harris, pp. 407-410; "Bands and distribution of the Eastern Shoshone," by E. Adamson Hoebel, pp. 410-413; "Wind River Shoshone Geography," by D.B. Shimkin, pp. 413-415. 1938

Rees, John E. *Idaho; Chronology, Nomenclature, Bibliography.* Conkey, 1918.

Ruby, Robert H. and John A. Brown. *Indians of the Pacific Northwest.* Univ. of Okla. Press. 1981

Schell, Frank R. *Ghost Towns and Live Ones; A Chronology of the Post Office Department in Idaho 1861-1973.* (Private print 1973). All rights purchased by Bert Webber, Webb Research Group, 1987

Schonchin, Lynn. *The Klamath Marsh.* Unpub ms. Chiloquin, Oregon. n.d.

Schoolcraft, Henry R. *Historical and Statistical Information, Respecting the History, Condition, and Prospects of the Indian Tribes of the United States.* 6 vols. Philadelphia. 1851-1857

Sheridan, Philip H. *Indian Fighting in the Fifties in Oregon and Washington Territories.* YeGalleon. 1987

Smith, Harriet L. *Camas, the Plant that Caused Wars.* Smith, Smith & Smith. 1978

Smith, Marian W. "Puyallup-Nisqually [Indians]." *Columbia University Contributions in Anthropology.* Vol. 32. NY. 1930

――――. "The Coast Salish of Puget Sound." *American Anthropology.* n.s., Vol. 43, No. 2. (Part 1) pp. 197-211. 1941

Spier, Leslie. "Tribal Distribution in Southwestern Oregon." *Oregon Historical Quarterly.* Vol. 28. No. 4. 1927

――――. "Klamath Ethnology." *University of California Publications in American Archaeology and Ethnology.* Vol. 30. pp. x + 1-388. University of California Press. 1930

――――. "Tribal Distribution in Washington." *American Anthropological Association General Services in Anthropology.* No. 3. 1936

――――. "Wishram Ethnology." *University of Washington Publications in Anthropology.* Vol. 3. 3, pp. 151-300. Seattle. 1930

Stevens, Isaac Ingals. *A True Copy of the Record of the Official Proceedings at Council in Walla Walla Valley 1855.* YeGalleon. 1985

Stone, Buena Cobb. *Fort Klamath; Frontier Post in Oregon 1863-1890.* Royal. 1964

Stowell, Cynthia D. *Faces of a Reservation [Warm Springs].* Oreg. Hist. Soc. Press. 1987

Suttles, Wayne. *Native Languages of the Northwest Coast.* (map). Oregon Historical Society. 1985

Swan, James G. *The Northwest Coast.* YeGalleon. 1966

Swanton, John R. *The Indian Tribes of North America.* [Smithsonian Institution Bureau of American Ethnology Bulletin 145] US Gov Print 0. 1953

――――. *Indian Tribes of Washington, Oregon & Idaho.* YeGalleon. 1968, 1979

Teit, James. "The Thompson Indians of British Columbia." *Memorial American Museum of Natural History.* Vol. 2. Publication of Jesup North Pacific Expedition Volume. 1. No. 4. Anthropology. Vol. 1. No. 4. N.Y. 1900

――――. "The Middle Columbia Salish." *University of Washington Publications in Anthropology.* Vol. 2. No. 4 pp. 38-128. Seattle. 1928

Teit, James, and Franz Boas. *The Salishan Tribes of the Western Plateaus.* [45th Annual Report Bureau of American Ethnology 1927-1928, Smithsonian. pp. 23-396] 1930

Thomas, Edward H. *Chinook, A History and Dictionary of the Northwest Coast Trade Jargon.* Metropolitan Press. 1935

Thompson, Erwin N. *Whitman Mission National Historic Site.* [No. 37 National Park Service Historical Handbook Series] Wash. D.C.

Trafzer, Clifford and Richard D. Scheuerman. *Renegade Tribe; The Palouse Indians of the Inland Pacific Northwest.* Wash. State U. Press. 1986

United States Coast Pilot 7, Pacific Coast. 18th Ed. U.S. Gov. Print Off. 1982

The United States Government Manual 1988/89. Office of the Federal Register, National Archives and Records Administration, U.S. Gov. Print. Office.

Urebenek, Mae. *Chief Washakie of the Shoshone.* Johnson. (Boulder Colo.) 1971

Walker, Deward E. *Indians of Idaho.* Univ. of Idaho Press. 1978

Walling, A.G. *History of Southern Oregon, Comprising Jackson, Josephine, Douglas, Curry and Coos Counties.* Walling. 1884

Wanapum Dam. (A paper discussing unique collection of history, artifacts, Indians) Grant County P.U.D., Ephrata. n.d.

Bibliography

Warning, John. *War on the Plains; Fort Mitchell on the Oregon-California Trail.* Ft. Mitchell Hist. Assn. (Inc.) 1988

Webber, Bert. *The Hero of Battle Rock.* (Expanded ed.) YeGalleon. 1973, 1974. Rev. Ed. 1978

_____. *Oregon Trail Emigrant Massacre of 1862 and Port-Neuf Muzzle-Loaders Rendezvous Massacre Rocks, Idaho.* Webb Research Gp. 1987

_____. *Postmarked Washington, An Encyclopedia of Postal History Covering Eleven Counties of Eastern Washington.* Vol. 1: Asotin, Spokane, Whitman Counties. YeGalleon. 1986

Webber, Bert and Margie Webber. *Beachcombing and Camping Along the Northwest Coast.* YeGalleon. 1978

_____. *Maimed by the Sea.* Erosion Along the Coasts of Oregon & Washington. YeGalleon. 1983

Wilkes, Charles. *Western America, Including California and Oregon, With Maps of Those Regions and of the Sacramento Valley.* Philadelphia. 1849

Wyoming: A Guide to History, Highways and People. Federal Writer's Project. W.P.A. Oxford. 1941

Yenne, Bill. *The Encyclopedia of North American Indian Tribes.* Arch Cape Press. 1986

Zucker, Jeff, Kay Hummel & Bob Hogfoss. *Oregon Indians Culture, History & Current Affairs.* Oregon. Hist. Society Press. 1983

MAPS AND CHARTS

Road Maps, official editions State Departments of Transportation:
British Columbia, Idaho, Illinois, Iowa, Minnesota, Montana, Nebraska, Oregon, Washington, Wyoming

U.S. Dept of Agriculture, U.S. Forest Service, maps of National Forests

U.S. Dept. of Commerce, Coast and Geodetic Survey, navigation charts

U.S. Dept. of Interior, Bureau of Land Management, maps.

Index

Index

Index

Index

207

ABOUT THE AUTHOR

BERT WEBBER is a research photojournalist who photographs and writes about the Pacific Northwest and the 19th century overland migration.

Webber graduated from Whitworth College in Spokane with emphasis in journalism then earned the Master of Library Science degree at University of Portland. He was a librarian in several schools in Washington and in Oregon. He sold his first commercially made photograph back in the late 1930s when still in high school in San Francisco. His writing is oriented to the "who, what, why, when, where" of the newspaper and he has seen hundreds of his spot-news stories and feature articles published. Many of his pieces have been in magazines and are listed in *The Reader's Guide to Periodical Literature.* In 1970 he retired from librarianship and went to full-time writing which he had been following earlier on a part-time basis. His first books, published by others, came out in 1973. Since then he has 28 titles of which 23 are currently in print.

Bert Webber is listed in *Who's Who in the West* and in *Contemporary Authors.* For a list of his books see "Author Index" to *Books in Print* in libraries and book stores.

Bert, with his wife Margie who has co-authored some of his books, lives in Oregon's Rogue River Valley.